THE TIMING
OF
MOTHERHOOD

THE TIMING
OF
MOTHERHOOD

by

CAROLYN AMBLER WALTER

Lexington Books

D.C. Heath and Company · Lexington, Massachusetts · Toronto

Library of Congress Cataloging-in-Publication Data

Walter, Carolyn Ambler.
The timing of motherhood.

Bibliography: p.
Includes index.
1. Motherhood—United States. 2. Maternal age—
United States. 3. Choice (Psychology) I. Title.
HQ759.W33   1986   306.8'743   85–45075
ISBN 0–669–11099–X (alk. paper)

Published simultaneously in Canada
Printed in the United States of America
Casebound International Standard Book Number: 0–669–11099–X
Library of Congress Catalog Card Number: 85–45075

The paper used in this publication meets
the minimum requirements of American National Standard
for Information Sciences–Permanence of Paper
for Printed Library Materials, ANSI Z39.48–1984.

ISBN 0-669-11099-X

The last numbers on the right below
indicate the number and date of printing.

10 9 8 7 6 5 4 3 2 1

95 94 93 92 91 90 89 88 87 86

Contents

Acknowledgments

MANY friends, colleagues, and relatives have provided the encouragement and help that I needed to finish this book—I thank all of you! A very special thank you goes to Francesca Giegengack, who served both as an editor and as a valuable source of emotional support throughout the writing of the book. Francesca's comments and insights as a woman, mother, and editor were invaluable in making this book an organized, readable work.

The comments and thoughts provided by eighty mothers comprise the heart of this book. I thank each of them for their willingness to share a part of their lives with me—and now with you, the reader.

During the research phase of this project, three Bryn Mawr faculty members, Philip Lichtenberg, Terry Carrilio, and Leslie Alexander, were particularly helpful. Since then, Arthur Schwartz, Carolyn Saari, Terry Hilt, and many of the students who have participated in my classes have provided insight and ideas.

Finally, to my family—John, Kim, Brian, and my mother—I owe a very special thanks for all of the warmth, love, and support they have provided. Kim and Brian have been patient when I was preoccupied with my work on the book, and John, my husband, has always been there for support, for a discussion of issues, and for a final bit of editing. Thus, this book is dedicated to my family, who have allowed me to grow in a very special way as a woman and as a mother.

THE TIMING
OF
MOTHERHOOD

1

Introduction

S INCE the late 1970s, there has been an important shift in the pattern of first births; more and more women are having their babies later and later in their lives. Demographers predict that within the next few years, there will be a 46 percent increase in the number of women having their first babies later in life. Simultaneously, there will be a decline in first births for younger women.[1] During the 1980s, women between the ages of 30 and 34 years are the only age group that has experienced a significant change in fertility rate. This increase in fertility for women in their early thirties, along with the recent stabilization of the birth rate in younger age groups, indicates that there is a continuing trend toward later childbearing.[2]

Several factors may account for this trend. For example, such advanced medical techniques as amniocentesis and chorionic villi sampling[3] make it more reasonable for women to consider motherhood later in life because they offer the chance to discover and terminate abnormal pregnancies. Furthermore, the women's movement has encouraged women to challenge traditional views and manage their biological clocks in terms of childbirth.

The timing of a first baby provides an excellent framework for understanding motherhood—its challenges and its contributions to adult personal growth. In this book, the process of mothering is viewed through the eyes of two groups of mothers who timed the births of their first children at different phases in their life cycles. One group had their first children early in adulthood (between the ages of 19 and 25); the other group delayed motherhood until at least age 30. These "delayers" had their first children between the ages of 30 and 41 and spent their early adult years (their twenties) focusing on their career development. The early-timing mothers focused their twenties on their children, husbands, and home.

Age provides a context for the marker events of adulthood, such as marriage, parenthood, and career; when we make choices, we embrace some experiences and give up others. Thus, early adulthood is a critical period for decision making, because choices made during this time are not easily reversed and will strongly influence the subsequent course of development.[4] The meaning of an important event such as parenthood is different for each person, depending on his or her stage of development. During specific phases of adulthood, certain tasks are more central and represent the focal point for the adult's attention. For example, during one's twenties, the primary task is separation from family of origin and establishment of a sense of competency; the task of one's thirties is to create one's own home base, to settle into a lifestyle, and to commit oneself to it.[5] How one accomplishes these tasks is affected by an important experience such as parenthood, and parenthood, in turn, is affected by the tasks on which one is working at the time.

It is more difficult for most women in American society to adjust to parenthood than to marriage or a job change,[6] and many women find motherhood more challenging than work outside the home.[7] The process of parenting confronts a mother with the paradoxical challenge of being available and "there" for her child but at the same time being sufficiently distant so that her child can separate and become an independent person. Motherhood is challenging in another sense, too; a woman must struggle to keep herself intact as a person while caring for her small child, who places many emotional demands on her. This book is written with the underlying belief that the growth and development of children affects the growth and development of their parents in important and exciting ways.

The ultimate task of life at any stage is to separate and declare our autonomy while connecting with and relating to others. The primary developmental task of adult life has been described as the integration of these two tensions, frequently referred to as *autonomy* and *homonomy*.[8] The integration of these tensions of adulthood is played out in the paradox of motherhood—the woman's capacity to connect with yet distance herself from her child. Thus, parenthood provides an opportunity for adults to balance the self–other tensions that are inherent in adult life.

My interest in studying the experiences of mothers grew out of my personal observations and my clinical work with mothers of preschool-aged children. The problems these mothers encountered with their small children centered on their struggle to preserve their own identities while meeting the pressing needs and demands of their children. These women were interested in exploring ways they might learn how to balance their own needs as adults with those of their children.

During discussions with these women, I was reminded of my own experiences as a new mother, at the age of 26, when I had the frightening feeling that I had lost my identity as a person. I remember that first year as a blur on the horizon. When I integrated my clinical observations with my own life experiences as the mother of two children, the idea for this book began to ferment. I became particularly curious about the interaction of the developmental growth of mother and child, in that they learn from and influence one another in fascinating ways.

Simultaneously, I observed an increase in the number of women I knew who were delaying childbirth well into their thirties. As I watched some of my older friends and neighbors coping with their children's preschool years, I observed that their struggle with parenthood somehow seemed different from that of the younger women with whom I had worked, as well as from my own experience as a new mother at age 26. These older women didn't seem to lose touch with themselves in the same way that I had observed in myself and other younger mothers. They seemed to celebrate their role as mother during the early years of their children's lives while still appreciating themselves as separate people. Although I enjoyed those first years as a mother, I'm not sure that I appreciated myself as a person—I was always searching for more and wondering what I was missing.

I wanted to understand the struggle of motherhood for both groups of women—those who timed the birth of their first children during their late teens and early twenties and those who waited until after thirty to have their first children. Where would I find similarities and differences between the two groups? I felt that I might be able to shed some light on what makes parenthood the most rewarding and yet the most frustrating of all occupations. By studying the experiences that women have as mothers in a very systematic way, I hoped to engender greater respect for the important role mothers play within our society.

The early chapters of this book provide a personality profile of each group of mothers, including the women's perceptions of themselves, how they cope with their daily activities, and their decision-making styles. Then the mothers discuss what they find most gratifying and frustrating about motherhood and share the ways in which they cope with some of their frustrations.

The women also discuss how they balance their own emotional needs with those of their small children. This appears to be the most challenging and frustrating aspect of parenthood, and it was the aspect on which early- and late-timing mothers differed most strikingly. For some mothers, meeting needs is a zero-sum game in which the child loses out if the mother meets her own needs. Other mothers recognize that a woman can cope with her role as a mother more effectively if she attends to her own needs as well as those of her children.

The mothers in my study wanted to discuss their social support networks: how their relationships with friends, husbands, and family are helpful or not helpful to them as parents and women; the ways in which motherhood has had an impact on their relationships with these important others; the characteristics of their family patterns; and whether husbands and wives share the work of the household and child care.

Next, the women who delayed childbirth to develop their careers discuss the ultimate balancing act—work and motherhood. Many of these women are questioning whether or not they really want to work at all or, if they do, how they can structure their lives so that work does not interfere with their relationships with their children. The reports from all the women interviewed clearly demonstrate that motherhood has a profound impact on the growth and development of women and on their self-esteem and self-confidence. Yet this impact is very different depending on the timing of parenthood.

Finally, the mothers discuss the advantages and disadvantages of timing parenthood when they did. On the basis of the findings of this study, I have tried to explore important implications for women and for society.[9] Women in this decade are clearly setting their own tone and developing a model for a lifestyle in which they hope to integrate their needs for affiliation and relationships with their needs for expressing autonomy and achievement.

I wrote this book for women—those who are thinking about becoming mothers and those who are already mothers and want to know about the experiences of other women. It is my hope that the discussions presented here—among both early- and late-timing mothers—will help women of all ages share their ideas and experiences and learn from one another. By no means do I intend to exclude men as readers; their roles as husbands and fathers will surely interest them in much of the subject matter. I expect, however, that women will relate more directly to the material, because they have actually lived the experiences, whereas a man's experience is limited to vicarious reflections. This book will also be helpful for professionals who work with women and mothers and for educators who are interested in life cycle issues.

From individual comments and group discussions, I have selected remarks that I believe are most typical of the women I interviewed. By reading this book, you are invited to join the discussions of the mothers, whose comments have provided the richest possible source of data. Just as the women who participated in my study felt supported and uplifted by the small-group experience—in which one person's shared experiences helped clarify or bolster those of another—perhaps you, the reader, will be touched in a similar way.

2

The Mothers:
Who They Are, How They Cope

Identity

What is it about you that makes you *you*? Your identity is the central core of what makes you unique. An individual's sense of identity has developed when she experiences a persistent sameness within herself and a sharing of that essential character with others.[1] Identity thus provides a consistency that characterizes the person and her reactions to others and events, despite the changes that occur over time and the many different roles she may play at any point in her life.

By the beginning of early adulthood (age 21 to 23) most people have some idea of how they will behave, relate, and feel under various circumstances. By this age, a person's behavior is also fairly predictable to others. How someone introduces herself or presents herself to others can provide a glimpse of how that person views or perceives herself—how she defines herself.

One of the most striking differences between the early-timing and late-timing mothers interviewed was the way in which they introduced themselves to other women during the small-group discussions. The women who had delayed childbirth described themselves in terms of both their role as a mother and their own achievements and accomplishments—through work or career, volunteer activities, or hobbies and interests. For these late-timers, motherhood is only part of their definition of themselves. It is almost as if they have chosen motherhood as a piece of the puzzle of life—something that complements the rest of their life. One 36-year-old mother's introduction of herself was typical of many others:

My name is Susan and I hope I can get through this, because my daughter who is two has been passing her cold back and forth. Everybody obviously has a work issue if they've waited to have a child. If somebody were eighteen or twenty or fresh out of college, they wouldn't have the same problems; but contrary to the others who've spoken here, I am completely, very avid about working. I started my own business—came to me as a complete surprise—very unplanned. After being so avid about having my own job, suddenly I have a completely relaxed position about working—I was a hobby person for about eleven years. My jobs were nearly hobbies until I decided to open my own business. Curiously enough, I'm trying to be a realist about trying to run a business and raise a child and consider having a second child. I'm in the considering stage and don't want to be like the generation of mothers before who were pretty much tennis and bridge players. I think there may be a happy compromise, and that's what I want to work out in the next three years.

However, for women who had their first children in their early twenties, motherhood is a larger share of their total identity. Their definitions of self focus more rigidly on their relationships with their children and their husbands. For example, during the small-group discussions, early-timing mothers rarely mentioned involvement in activities other than motherhood when they introduced themselves to other group members. One woman, who had her first child at 22, introduced herself to the group in this way:

My name is Sally and I have two little boys—one almost four and one who is seven months this week. I worked outside of the home in the nursing profession before I had kids. I tried working with children but it's too time consuming on top of mothering. So, my principal job is taking care of and entertaining two children. One is in nursery school, so that it is a little bit of help.

Studies of adult female development reveal two divergent personality patterns among young women. One pattern is described as a personal or self-defined sense of identity; the other is a more reflected, social sense of identity. One researcher found that women who were career-oriented before motherhood seem to retain a personal sense of identity that is determined by their own accomplishments and in their own terms—the self is viewed apart from others. This personal identity, which involves an awareness of and an emphasis on the person's talents, capabilities, and needs,[2] is similar to Andras Angyal's conception of *autonomy,* in which the person is focused on self-determination, mastery, and achievement—the need to advance one's interests by bending the environment to suit one's needs.[3] Thus, autonomy involves the processes of taking charge and caring for the self; it is tied to achievement needs or mastery.[4]

There are some indications that women who remain full-time home-makers or who return to employment after child rearing are more likely to develop a reflected sense of identity. They experience a moratorium on the development of a personal identity until their children reach school age. A reflected or social identity has an external focus in that there is an emphasis on "significant others in one's life, rather than on one's personal characteristics."[5] For these women, identity formation is based more on association with others than on their own accomplishments. The self-esteem and feelings of worth among this group of women derived from their participation in the lives of significant others.

This reflected or socially defined sense of identity seems related to Andras Angyal's conception of *homonomy*—a trend within the individual that motivates her to fit herself to her environment and to share and participate in something that is larger than the individual self. The person submerges her individuality by becoming part of a social group, community, or relationship. This trend, which is expressed in a desire for love and interpersonal relationships, is related to concepts of merging, communion, contact, belonging, affiliation, and dependence.[6] It manifests itself in being at one with other people and in the lack of separations.[7]

Late-timing mothers in this study worked an average of 9 years—almost three times the number of years early-timing mothers had worked (3.5 years) before the birth of their first children (see table 1; please note that all tables are in the appendix). On the Adjective Checklist to Describe Personality (see tables 2 and 3), the latetiming mothers described themselves as more achievement-oriented, autonomous, self-reliant, and individualistic in personality than the early-timing mothers did.

However, although the late-timing mothers perceived themselves as more autonomous than the early-timing mothers did, they also described themselves as emotional, nurturing, sympathetic, and supportive. Their sense of identity appears to be both personal and social. This finding may support the development of a new model for women—one in which the woman is able to balance a high need for achievement and autonomy with a high need for nurturing and dependence.

The personality profile of the early-timing mothers is clearly more one-dimensional than that of the late-timing mothers. On the Adjective Checklist to Describe Personality, the early-timers described themselves as compliant, self-subordinating, gentle, and supportive, but rarely autonomous or achievement-oriented (see table 3).

The women who participated in this study were asked on a questionnaire to rank four factors (own achievements, relationship with husband, relationship with child/children, perception of parental support for me and my role) that they perceived to be most important in determining their sense of self. Early-timing mothers more frequently ($p < .01$) chose "my relationship with my husband" as the most important factor, whereas significantly more late-timing mothers ($p < .00001$) perceived that their own achievements (hobbies, work, school, volunteer activities) had been more important to their sense of self (see table 4).[8]

Decision-Making Styles

One of the most striking ways in which the early- and late-timing mothers differed was in their methods of coping with daily activities and decision making. On the questionnaire, early- and late-timing mothers gave different ranks to factors influencing their decisions in daily activities or work. Late-timers more frequently chose their "own needs" as most influential in daily decision making, whereas early-timers more frequently chose "my children's needs" as the most important factor (see table 5). Just as external relationships are more important determinants of the identity of younger women, the needs of others are more important factors in their decision making. In contrast, late-timers more often base their sense of identity and the source of their decision-making styles on their own "internal barometers" and their own needs. This is not to say that they neglect the needs of their children and families in their decision making, but the focus is different.

It was also evident that whereas late-timing mothers felt in charge of their lives and time and were confident about the decisions they made, the lives of the early-timing mothers were primarily determined by others. For example, before going out at night to a meeting or some other activity, early-timers felt the need to get their husbands' approval. As one 25-year-old mother with two young children reported poignantly:

> Whenever I want time to myself, I have to check with my husband first and make sure it's OK—he doesn't check with me though.

It is striking that no late-timing mother ever reported that she felt she needed to obtain approval from her husband before engaging in an activity of pleasure for herself.

A major theme that emerged during group sessions with early-timers was worrying about whether they were "doing it [mothering] right." They reported much difficulty in trusting themselves and their decisions. This self-doubt revealed itself as a critical factor in problems of discipline and in ambivalent feelings about leaving their children with others. Early-timers expressed an extreme sense of responsibility around "making or breaking" their child with each decision they made. They consistently questioned whether they were doing the right thing. One mother's statement is characteristic of this indecisiveness and worrying:

> That's what I find difficult—not knowing whether something feels right or not—that and worrying when they're sick. They've been sick and you've been up five times during the night and you check them and you worry and call the doctor and when their fever does get high and you feel guilty and didn't call the doctor—you think about the other times when you did call and it was nothing. It's the worrying over that and then the discipline. You never know if you're handling their problem the right way or not. My older daughter has been crabby all weekend—crying spells—I put up with it for so long and then you get aggravated and you say "If you don't stop this . . ."
>
> You never know if you're doing the right thing—you always worry. Did I handle this problem right or is this a stage? Am I doing the right thing? This is what drives me crazy about motherhood—all the wondering and the worrying.

Another young mother expressed her uncertainty about leaving her 2-year-old-child:

> Just worrying—that drives me crazy. How far should you push your child? My two-year-old won't stay with anybody, and last year at the end I stayed home all summer. Then when I started to go crazy, I just left her and let her scream and she shut up in time, but at the beginning I thought, "Oh, I'm abandoning my child," but after a whole summer I had to get out. My mother said she'd watch her. She still pulls that stunt now and then and after I leave everybody says she's fine. You never know—Is that right? Is that how to handle that problem? Do you stay home with them or do you go out and say the heck with them—they'll learn how to live with it? Nobody tells you the right or wrong answer to that.

The late-timing mothers rarely discussed their uncertainty or worry about coping with their children. They seem to sense that they are right about certain issues, and they don't question themselves as much as the early-timing mothers. (Perhaps these women are unable to view themselves as being "wrong." This may be an area of vulnerability as well as a strength.)

The ratings of responses from early-timing mothers indicated that they lacked trust in their own decisions and needed to "check them out" with others in their lives before making a final decision.

During small-group discussions, early-timers tended to seek support from others in the group before making a comment, finished sentences for one another, and interpreted meanings for one another. In small groups, the early-timing mothers frequently waited for acceptance from one another before making comments. As a group, they were less able to allow differences to surface among them regarding attitudes and viewpoints toward parenthood. Early-timing mothers also had difficulty staying with the task of answering and discussing questions during group sessions.

In contrast, late-timers had little difficulty focusing on the task of answering and discussing questions during the group sessions. These women were much less dependent on the researcher, and questions rarely had to be reframed or refocused; the discussions tended to flow more easily. There was evidence from overt group behavior that the late-timing mothers experienced greater ease and comfort in coping with the task of group membership, which requires an ability to connect with others while preserving one's sense of autonomy.[9] In general, the early-timers have not developed their sense of autonomy to the same degree as late-timing mothers have.

Coping with Daily Activities

Clinical observations by the researchers and the raters indicated that late- and early-timing mothers showed marked differences in the way they perceive and cope with their world. For late-timing mothers, planning, organization, and structure are critical to their daily functioning, and motherhood is viewed as a goal-directed, purposeful activity. Late-timers use their capacity for organization and their ability to structure their lives as a way of coping with the stresses of motherhood. They are successful in planning their days and meeting some of their own needs as well as those of their children. As one mother said:

> Planning is an important issue. We waited seven years, deliberately—very planned. I wonder what it would have been like if we had accidentally gotten pregnant and muddled through. Instead, you have this special thing that you've waited for—it's like a project. You planned it and now here it is—if it doesn't turn out right, what then? Because of being older, we knew our interests and knew what was important to us.

Another late-timer said: "I run my house just like I run my business. I have an appointment book." During the small-group discussions, one of the other late-timers responded to this comment:

> You turned it into a business. I wanted to but I couldn't. I couldn't get any-
> thing done at home. I stayed in pajamas and watched TV. I had to do some-
> thing. I knew I didn't want to go back to work but needed something. I found
> volunteer work and have a calendar and run it like a business. I have to fill my
> day and I have to do it in an organized manner. If you've lived an organized life
> ten years and you choose to stay home and can find things to do at home that
> you enjoy to fill the time, then you do end up running your home like a busi-
> ness. Things had to be organized at the office. Now that I'm home I feel very
> organized—my need that I got from working is to accomplish something—even
> if it's laundry.

Although this ability to plan and organize one's life can be helpful in parenting, it can also have drawbacks. The late-timers expressed some diffi-culty accommodating children in a well-established relationship with their husbands and their well-established household routines. The strong em-phasis on planning and organization displayed by most late-timers can lead to a lack of spontaneity and difficulty in coping with the chaos of life with children. Because they are accustomed to planning their schedules and daily activities according to their own needs, late-timing mothers may find it more difficult to be flexible when coping with the changes and impulsivity that a child brings to the lives of a married couple. Several women mentioned not wanting to have "a house full of kids," as they'd "spent a lot of time and money collecting lovely furniture" and didn't want it damaged.

In response to the question, "What are the most difficult aspects of motherhood for you?" one mother replied:

> Having another person in the house—contending with another will in a house
> where two very willful people live. We were married several years—we were
> ready and planned our child but we got used to doing things when we wanted.
> We thought, of course, our child would blend right in—we'd make him blend
> in. We found out that we had to blend in. I see as difficult the meshing of
> personalities and time schedules—being up all night.

On another level, some late-timers reported that their need to plan and structure their time has some disadvantages for them socially. One mother, who was 32 when her daughter was born, commented:

We may be making some of our own problem. I have to plan everything. We are so structured in our own social lives. I spend time figuring out whether Susan should go there—social obligations. I don't have the flexibility that if I were younger and I lived in spontaneous neighborhoods I would have. You are older and fussier. Houses have nicer furniture and you want to preserve things. We may turn off the support system a little bit. While being organized may be good for us, it may cut off the support system.

At the same time, this ability to structure and organize their lives seems to help these mothers cope with the stresses of parenthood. As noted in chapter 5, the late-timer's capacity to plan her days successfully helps her obtain some personal space for herself, which, in turn, enables her to cope with the dual task of motherhood—meeting her own needs and those of her children.

In contrast to the more organized style of late-timing mothers, early-timing mothers were perceived by the researchers and raters as having more spontaneity and less deliberation in their style of relating to the world and to others. This tendency is revealed in their descriptions of how they decided to become parents. One early-timer said: "We felt like we were ready." Another said: "I just wanted one—I wanted to have a baby—that's all there was to it." Still another young mother added:

One of the biggest decisions to have a baby is just that you get that sudden urge that you have to have a baby—there wasn't any explanation—it was just one of those things—a calling.

This style contrasts with that of late-timing mothers, for whom having a child is more of a "rational, planned project." For early-timing mothers, having a baby is part of the natural order—something that happens to them when they are ready. This tendency toward being more flexible in daily routines was revealed by one early-timing mother:

I am still fairly rigid, but with children you just can't be that way—if you run your house like the Navy runs a ship, I think that would drive everyboby crazy—the household would fall apart.

This statement is in direct contrast to those made by late-timing mothers, who carefully planned and scheduled their time, even going so far as using appointment books.

For the early-timing mothers, planning and organization is less critical. These mothers tend to "go with the flow" of the activity and behavior of their children and their husbands. Going with the flow of activity in the household helps them cope with the early months of childhood, when mother and child need to be merged in a rather tight unit so that the mother can effectively mirror the infant's responses. However, the tendency of early-timers to focus on the other person and to allow their lives to be more determined by others causes problems for them in asserting and securing their own needs for autonomy and personal space.

It appears that late-timing mothers have derived a sense of self from their own achievements and consequent feelings of competency. They have developed the capacity to know themselves as women who can function autonomously. In effect, they can count on themselves and take care of themselves.

Some women who had decided to delay childbirth reported that they did so because they observed their own mothers' lives revolving around them when they were children. These late-timers observed that this made life adjustment very difficult for their own mothers once their children had left home. The late-timing mothers I interviewed did not want to get caught in this way, so they chose to have their work lives more organized and settled before the birth of their first child. As one 34-year-old lawyer with a 2-year-old daughter commented:

> Looking at my mother and the way life revolved around kids—she had difficulty when we left knowing what to do with herself. She had a difficult time when the kids left home. I don't want to be in a situation like that. I wanted to make sure I got things organized enough before I stopped to have kids, so I'll have something to go back to.

Another late-timer compared the way she has handled the timing of parenthood in her own life with that of her mother, who had her children during her early twenties:

> But look what happened to all of our mothers. I have a lot of friends whose mothers devoted themselves to their children exclusively—some of them paid for it dearly—everything for the child. They wouldn't buy a dress for themselves. I can remember my mother didn't look very glamorous and she didn't have any interests other than the PTA. Many of them found themselves without husbands because they [husbands] were tired of seeing a lady who spent everything on their kids and nothing on themselves and didn't know anything. Today's woman has a different expectation—"Wait a minute; I don't want to go this far. I have to take care of myself, too. I have to read and have some time for myself. I have to pay attention to me."

The late-timing mothers who planned their lives differently from those of their mothers had decided to take time to develop themselves first as individuals, recognizing the extreme difficulty in doing so once parenthood intrudes.

Furthermore, late-timers have developed multiple roles via their work, career, or other outside interests, and they can therefore choose a more varied lifestyle while mothering a preschool child. They may be less likely to be so dependent on their children as a source of support for their self-esteem. Other researchers have found that multiple roles may be a source of satisfaction, not fragmentation, even when young women are concerned with young children.[10]

Summary

The reports from late-timing mothers suggest that their sense of identity is both personal and social. For them, motherhood represents a smaller share of their identity than it is for early-timers, whose sense of self is more social and is closely intertwined with their relationships with their children and husbands. Early-timers tend to view their children as extensions of themselves.

Late-timers plan and structure their time more carefully. Although this style has advantages, in that it preserves their autonomy while caring for a small child, late-timers report that they have some difficulty fitting their children into a well-established household routine. Early-timers seem less organized in their approach to life, which helps them "go with the flow" of a busy household. However, this style may make it more difficult for the mother to carve out some space for herself during the day.

3

The Gratifications and Frustrations of Motherhood

MOTHERHOOD is an experience that can be, at one and the same time, both gratifying and frustrating for the woman who chooses it. During the preschool years, as the child moves in and out of an emotionally and physically intimate relationship with the mother, the mother must repeatedly adjust to ongoing changes in the child's relationship with her. At every stage of development, the mother must be sensitive to what her children need and to when the children are ready and able to distance themselves from her.

This process is stressful because, during the preschool years, children may perceive themselves at one minute as merged with mother but at the next minute as separate—and mother as dangerous. It is easy for the mother to get caught between maternal overprotection (maintaining the child's dependence too long) and maternal deprivation (making premature demands on her child's autonomy).

Many important theorists have pointed to the critical need for mothers to protect and hold their young children while the children are developing yet to allow the children freedom to explore as much of the environment as they are capable of exploring.[1] Thus, as the child is moving through critical stages of symbiosis and separation/individuation, the mother must be able to "hold on" and "let go" appropriately. Too much holding on has deleterious consequences, as does the granting of too much—or premature—autonomy. Mothering is a slow process, involving oscillations between merging or immersion and autonomy.

Margaret Mahler has observed that mothers vary in their responses to specific maturational events in the development of their preschool children. Whereas some mothers are more comfortable with the symbiotic phases, in which child and mother are closely connected both physically and emotionally, other mothers express greater comfort when the child becomes more independent.[2] It seems possible that women who were in different stages of adult development at the time their first children were born might respond differently to the phases of symbiosis and separation/individuation in their children's development.

The Gratifications of Motherhood

Late-Timing Mothers Enjoy Merging and Autonomy

To discover how a mother responds to changes in her child's demands on her, the women were asked to describe (via the questionnaire and group discussions) the most pleasurable or satisfying aspects of parenthood and the most difficult or frustrating aspects. The responses during the group interviews corroborated the questionnaire data and explained them in greater depth.

In the open-ended questionnaire, late-timing mothers expressed as much satisfaction with activities of mothering that encouraged merging or connecting with the child as with more autonomous activities that allowed for some emotional distance. For late-timing mothers, almost half (49 percent) of the ratable responses were coded in the category indicating their comfort with merging or closeness with their children, and the remainder (51 percent) were coded in the category indicating their comfort with activities in which their children were autonomous or separated from them.

For example, when asked about the most pleasurable aspect of motherhood, one mother responded "The warmth and love in my relationship with my child." Many late-timing mothers considered the nursing experience a highlight of their role as a parent. As one mother commented, "The period of child rearing that was especially satisfying for me was the first year, when I was nursing."

Late-timing mothers also reported much pleasure and enjoyment in watching their children's development or in responding to their verbal behavior. This response indicates an enjoyment of the child's autonomy as well as the mother's comfort in having some emotional distance from the child. As one 34-year-old woman reported her most satisfying moments as a mother:

> Most recently [her child is 11 months old], when I feel that my daughter's increasing ability to communicate/understand/verbalize has been a really pleasurable experience for me.

Two other late-timers also indicated their extreme pleasure in their children's growth and independence:

> Currently, child rearing (my child is two and one-half) has been most satisfying—my children are becoming independent of me for many basic needs and are good communicators and companions. It is very exciting to be able to enjoy activities together and discuss their feelings and ideas.

> Most current year—children are six and four—I love watching their development; each year they get better and better. As they get older and are away from home more, my life incorporates more activity which refreshes me emotionally.

Furthermore, the comments of late-timing mothers more frequently indicated that they seemed to receive equal satisfaction from being close to their children as from being more autonomous and separate from them—an indication they had balanced these tensions. Two mothers who were over 30 when their first children were born reported their most satisfying moments of motherhood:

> Watching my daughter learn a new skill, hearing her giggle, listening to her stories—seeing her being busy and happy. I also love the hugs and kisses and just cuddling with her.

> Raising a daughter who is strong and independent; cuddling babies and toddlers.

It is significant that there were no such responses from the early-timing mothers. None of them indicated both extreme pleasure with physical and emotional closeness to a child and extreme pleasure with separation. Although late-timing mothers enjoyed the early months, when there was more of a "bodily tie" to the child, these same mothers also responded with pleasure to the new relationship with the child who can separate from the mother. These women often remarked that they enjoyed the company or companionship of a child at the toddler stage. As one 36-year-old mother commented to a group of seven other late-timing mothers: "We're all intrigued with the spirit of these kids."

Early-Timing Mothers Enjoy Being Physically and Emotionally Close to Their Children

Responses from early-timing mothers demonstrated their comfort with being closely connected with their children. Three-quarters of their questionnaire responses clustered around two statements on the rating scheme that indicated comfort with being physically and emotionally connected to their child. Only one-quarter of their responses clustered around statements indicating comfort with autonomy and separation. One of the trained raters who analyzed the responses from early-timing mothers during the group discussions commented that, for these women:

> Motherhood is viewed as an opportunity for physical closeness. Child-oriented activities are viewed as total immersion into children, as loss of relationship with spouse, and as an enjoyment of the child's total dependence upon them.

Two young mothers replied as follows when asked what was most pleasurable about motherhood for them:

> Babies—caring for specific needs—being able to understand and respond to nonverbal messages. I've tried to be as receptive as I can to another person's feelings and needs.

> When my son or daughter says, "I love you Mommy," just out of the clear blue. When they kiss me without me asking for a kiss. When they seem happy and smile. We stress loving and sharing in teaching the children.

The following comment, by a woman who was 23 when her first child was born, clearly demonstrates the importance of being close to her child in a very physical way:

> From the first time I heard the baby's heartbeat in the womb—kicking inside the womb—first time I held her in my arms after delivery—at delivery the way she responded to my voice when I talked to her, the first time I nursed her.

Early-Timing Mothers May View Their Children as Extensions of Themselves

Although women who timed the birth of their first children early in adulthood expressed more comfort with the earliest stages of the child's life, when the physical and emotional demands for merging with the child are greatest, there was evidence that these same mothers more readily view their children as extensions of themselves. Their comments indicate the degree to which these mothers value being needed and loved by their children.

The two raters who analyzed the data noted that a major theme in the responses of early-timing mothers was the importance of children in their lives. The raters also observed that the children appear to provide a basic support for their mothers' sense of well-being and identity. One rater commented:

Children are more important than the spouse in this period of child rearing. There is no spousal cooperation, and it is almost as if the spousal relationship is put on hold. There is a focus on intimacy with children and enjoyment of dependency of children—less differentiation of self from children. There is less time taken for self—less sense of self as a person distinct from that of a mother—as if their individuality is temporarily put on hold, too.

For these early-timing mothers, who enjoy being needed and loved by their children, parenthood is more of a "calling." As one woman voiced this:

It's nice to be really needed and loved by someone—I think the children are the ones that give you the most of that—you really feel that you're important in their lives—my husband is important but not in the same way that the children are. [I asked her to describe how it is different.] I just think that it's very important as a mother to have that feeling—their needing you and wanting you—and I think the children show that very much.

It can be seen from the responses of the women in this group that these young mothers enjoyed the very early years of child rearing (especially infancy), when they felt that they had more control over their children and their lives. A brief excerpt from a group session with early-timers reveals this attitude:

Now I come into the house and it's a hurricane—now they're not out and in as much, but then when they come home it's a joke—they have to eat all the time. They're not in here more than one minute when they're dumping this or that. I think it was easier when they were babies.

That's because you had control.

That's right, I had control. I carried one around on my hip and one would take a nap—for some reason I got it done.

These mothers also displayed a tendency to measure their own self-esteem in terms of their children's actions. When asked what she considered the most difficult things about being a mother, one young mother commented:

When one of them doesn't act right—when company comes and they act their worst—then you wonder, "What am I doing wrong?" If they're angels, I feel that I must be doing something right—it flip flops back and forth for me, depending on how they're acting. I find myself wondering if there is something inside me that they're picking up on—are they reacting to me? I'm kind of mixed up.

As noted earlier, early-timing mothers rely on others for their source of self-esteem and have focused their early adult years on meeting the needs of home and family. These mothers may be most comfortable during the earliest months of their children's lives because being needed by a child enhances their self-esteem. Several early-timing mothers claimed that their children perceived them as "close to God"—an expression never used by the late-timing mothers in this study. The following statements from early-timing mothers reflect the importance of motherhood for their self-esteem:

Being needed and loved by my children makes life more valuable to me—and has made me more aware of my creator.

I feel good about myself because I feel my kids are basically good—I enjoy being with my kids—I also enjoyed nursing—seeing your children become good and sweet.

Being needed by their children is very important to these young women, because being a mother is a large part of how they define themselves as adults. As one young mother commented:

Having a child means that baby loves you—they're extremely attached. Most of your other relationships have been different; the adoration you get from your child is different from others—you're a god to them—it's really good for the ego.

Thus, for these younger mothers, parenthood is a significant portion of their total identity as women. They more readily view their children as extensions of themselves, and they need their children to bolster their self-esteem.

It is significant that none of the late-timing mothers indicated that being needed by her child enhanced her own self-esteem. For late-timing mothers, parenthood is a smaller part of their self-definition. Before becoming mothers, they established a firmer sense of who they are. They can count on themselves and do not get lost so easily in the merging of mother and child. On an emotional level, late-timers seem to understand that an intense closeness with their children does not require that they give up their own sense of who they are. From the small-group discussions, it was clear that late-timing mothers, though trained for employment or careers that interested them, were pleased to be focusing on their roles as mothers—so long as they can sustain other, nonchild interests. Thus, although late-timing mothers enjoy and are involved in their role as mothers, they are also able to separate themselves from this role. Though deeply invested in motherhood, they are able to perceive themselves as functioning in roles other than that of mother.

The Frustrations of Motherhood

Early-timing and late-timing mothers expressed very different opinions regarding what is most difficult or frustrating about being a mother. Whereas early-timing mothers considered discipline and separating from their children among their greatest frustrations, late-timing mothers found the lack of free time to pursue their own interests most difficult for them.

Early-Timing Mothers Struggle with Discipline and Separation

One 26-year-old mother with two children, aged 2 and 4, reported the most difficult and frustrating aspect of motherhood for her:

> From the period starting with teething until [an unknown time]. It was my first experience where I really didn't know how to handle situations. I was confused re my own feeling about discipline—I had seen how other mothers had started physically disciplining babies. It took me a long time to be comfortable with my negative feelings toward the baby.

Statistical anlysis of the questionnaire data indicates that significantly more (ANOVA, $p < .01$) of the early-timing mothers reported the most frustrating aspects of motherhood as activities that reflect their difficulties in encouraging their children's independence and their discomfort in separating from their children (maintaining both physical and emotional distance). The responses of two early-timing mothers illustrate this finding:

> Discipline—being a first-time mother. I'm learning how to be an effective disciplinarian and sometimes I fail miserably. I have a child who screams.

When they don't listen to me and then turn around and do as they like. When I just finish saying, "Don't do that."

It is difficult for many early-timing mothers to discipline a child and set appropriate limits, because they feel unsure of themselves and question whether or not they are handling things in the "right way." Motherhood creates problems in this arena because setting limits and enforcing appropriate discipline requires establishment of a certain emotional distance between mother and child. This is a particularly difficult task when a mother's own identity is so intertwined with that of her child's. This intense merger of mother and child can make such tasks particularly stressful because the mother is afraid of the child's anger and may fear that the child will reject her when she delimits the child's behavior. During a small-group discussion, this problem was further elaborated, and the confusion these young mothers experience became more apparent:

> I find it difficult to find a punishment to fit the crime. The kind of punishment that relates to what they've done. Sometimes I rack my brains trying to think of something to get the message across about what they're doing—that their punishment is trying to clue them in to what they've done that is wrong. I just can't think of anything, so you end up with this goofy punishment. Maybe it gets across, but I find it difficult to think of the right thing to do. And then when my husband and I agree on what punishments we should dish out, he'll come out with this cooky punishment. I'd like to say, "What are you giving him that punishment for?—it doesn't make sense to me."

> The discipline is the hardest thing for me. You never know if you're really right or not. I'll say "Pick up the toy and put it in the box," and she is fussing. I think, "Am I accomplishing anything? Should I have just put her up for her nap and do it myself?" You never know if you're right or wrong.

In the following comment by a young mother of a 10-month-old baby and a 3-year-old, it is striking how difficult it is for this mother to cope with the baby's need for some separation and distance from the mother:

> The hardest thing for me (I also wrote this down on my questionnaire), going from where she is now, is not wanting to hit the baby and having all these bad feelings toward her. When the baby hits you in the face—I didn't want to hit her but I was frustrated because I really had a hard time dealing with my feelings toward her and being comfortable spanking her on the bottom—I was so afraid to hit her. It came to the point for me that every kid gets hit on the

backside and hollered at—but it took at least six months battling with my feelings about it. A few people I saw with little kids—I knew I didn't want to do
what they did—but I didn't see anybody do what I felt was right for me.

A 26-year-old mother who has three small children—4½, 3, and 2—
revealed her struggle with discipline:

The most difficult thing for me is that I'm not fond of the way I was raised—
lots of corporal punishment. I wonder if the way I'm disciplining them is the
same or different. I don't want my children to have any fear of me the way I
have a fear of my family. I love my parents and they're great with the kids, but
I was afraid of them—afraid of them seeing my report card. The difficulty is
discipline, but I just want to make sure the way I discipline doesn't make them
afraid of me. Recently, some friend of mine gave me tips on discipline. I don't
know whether to smack them on the hiney or sit them down and talk to them.
Am I disciplining them right? Is there a right way to discipline them? . . . Big
thing is discipline because I want to be a real good friend of theirs when they
get older. I can't go to my mother with a problem and I want them to be able
to come to me.

This mother's struggle is related to how she was disciplined by her parents
during her own childhood. Early-timing mothers are at a stage in their adulthood when they are still coping with individuating from their families of
origin. They are therefore vulnerable around issues of separation with regard
to their children as well as making their own way in the world as separate
adults.

It is significant that late-timing mothers rarely mentioned discipline as a
problem for them in coping with the tensions of parenthood. This may be
because these mothers are more able to distance themselves emotionally
from their children and do not view their children's negative behavior as
personal attacks on them. They may separate more easily because they are
not struggling so hard with this issue in their own adult lives, having integrated some of this learning during their twenties.

Early-timing mothers also evidenced discomfort and guilt about separating
from their children. One 24-year-old mother of two daughters, aged 2½ and
3½, commented on this conflict:

I worry about stupid things, too. I spent the day away from them yesterday,
and they're not newborns, but I've been away from them before. I knew that
they were spending the entire day away with someone else and thought of all
the horrible things that could happen to them while they were away. Then I

thought "This is ridiculous—go out and enjoy yourself," but you just keep worrying anyway. I heard once before that a mother never thinks that anyone can take care of her children as well as she can. I knew this woman who was taking care of my children had raised her own two kids, and my husband would be with them part of the time I was gone. But I kept thinking that they were going to be in the car part of the time and maybe something would happen there—they'd get sick. Stupid things—but I kept worrying about them.

This woman agreed with other mothers in the group that worrying and wondering about motherhood is one of its greatest difficulties.

Early-timing mothers also expressed concern about their lack of confidence in themselves or in being sure that what they do is right. (Some of the comments about discipline also support this.) One early-timing mother noted the most frustrating aspect of parenthood for her:

To know what is best for my child in the long run. Knowing that I keep making mistakes along the way and hoping they're not too serious.

In addition, the early-timing mother experiences a great deal of difficulty coping with her child's illness—her own sense of helplessness and the uncertainty that comes with illness. Two young mothers reported this as the most difficult aspect of parenthood for them:

The kids are sick and no better even after tests: the fear of the unknown.

Not being able to take their pain away when they are sick—not being able to transfer that pain to myself.

The young mother struggles with her child's growing need for independence and assertion of the child's own identity. Her child's thrust toward autonomy and separation may arouse unresolved conflicts regarding her own separation issues, and these conflicts may increase her discomfort in coping with similar issues in her child's development.

Furthermore, women who time their first babies early in their own adult development may respond to their children's push toward separation and growth as a loss of dependence on a close-knit relationship with their children. They may not comprehend this change as a growth in the mother-child relationship. Furthermore, for these mothers—who tend to define being separate as being alone—there may be increased vulnerability to depression due to fear of loss of attachment to the child. This new relationship with the child may also signal a loss of identity for them. In the following comments, two young mothers in their mid-twenties reveal how difficult this issue is for them:

> The most difficult time for me was when my kids were ages three and three and one-half, because it just seemed like overnight that my daughter changed into a little person with a mind of her own and at times will not take any direction without a battle.

> When my oldest child was three to three and one-half and was trying to become such an independent child—all negative behavior—very defiant.

Late-Timing Mothers Want More Time for Themselves

Late-timing mothers rarely expressed concern regarding disciplining or separating from their children. Rather, the late-timers expressed pleasure and enjoyment at having some time away from their children—time that most of them scheduled on a regular basis. As discussed in chapter 5, this ease in separating from her child allows the late-timing mother to meet some of her own emotional needs and those of the marital relationship. During a group discussion with eight other late-timing mothers, one 38-year-old woman commented:

> You don't realize sometimes that you should get out on a regular basis. I was getting into a rut. I love my children, but we went away this past summer for four days without our children and we discovered a whole new world—all by ourselves. It was like years ago when we were first married and it was just the two of us. It's something that you really have to organize to do, even though you may not want to do it at first.

All the group members agreed. The late-timers reported that the most difficult aspect about motherhood for them is not having enough time for themselves to pursue their own activities. This expresssion of difficulty with not having time for themselves reflects a desire to be separate and autonomous from their children. It may also represent vulnerability regarding merging or closeness, which mirrors the larger issue with which these late-timers are struggling within their adult lives. One 38-year-old mother noted the most frustrating aspect of parenting for her:

> Giving up those hours of private time for myself and time once reserved for myself and husband.

Another late-timer commented:

> Not having enough time to do things for myself, like projects around the house (painting).

Other late-timers reported a great deal of frustration in balancing their time with both career and family responsibilities. These women also experienced frustration regarding the intrusion and disruption of parenthood on their capacity for planning their daily schedules. The following comments illustrate this cluster of responses:

> Frustration and tension in trying to reconcile a demanding job that is supposed to be part-time and having free time to relax and play with my child; the disruption of my daily schedule.

> Since I tend to keep extremely busy, when something unplanned occurs— unexpected guests, illness, lack of sleep—my patience and tolerance become short.

For Late-Timers, The Early Months of Parenthood Can Be Difficult

The following comments by late-timing mothers indicate that they found the early stage of parenthood (the first 3 months) difficult because of the burden of having someone so dependent on them:

> The infant/toddler stage was the most difficult for me—physically and psychologically—the constant demands, whining, and continued caretaking.

> My most difficult time was during my child's first two months. He cried a considerable amount and of course needed constant attention. I found this period physically and emotionally draining.

However, one of the real frustrations for late-timers that occurs during the first 3 months of their children's lives relates to the tension they experience when they do not feel they are "stimulating their child" or are "being stimulated by the child." Late-timers miss the positive verbal feedback that was structured into the jobs they had before motherhood. This verbal feedback was important in building their self-esteem. These mothers also lament the opportunity to accomplish goals during infancy, when their babies are demanding so much attention. Frequently, these women commented, "I can't accomplish much." One mother summed it up well:

For me, the initial part is hard—all of a sudden you have this tremendous responsibility for a whole other person, and that in itself makes the whole experience strained. You're not getting enough sleep—no feedback—plus many visitors, and for some reason I could never get anything accomplished—I was shoving dishes in the trash. It was a very hard time. I had read so much regarding how important those first years are and what to do. I realized that everything I did would have enormous impact later on my son for the rest of his life. That in itself is a lot to carry around. . . . I had lots of advice.

Related to this difficulty resulting from lack of verbal feedback and their inability to accomplish goal-oriented tasks is their apparent discomfort in playing with their children. Several late-timers who reported difficulty playing with their children felt that it was because they were older and that this aspect of parenting would have been easier if they had had their children earlier in their adult lives. The following comments illustrate these feelings:

I'll play verbal games, but to get down on the floor and play Legos is not my thing.

I'm afraid that once you start playing with them, they're going to want you to play with them all the time. I can't be my kids' playmate.

I put my daughter in nursery school because I felt I was not a good playmate for her. I don't enjoy doing it—I don't do it well.

Thus, late-timing mothers focus on verbal communication with their children and find less enjoyment in nonverbal, childlike activities. There appears to be a need for these mothers to have more stimulation in their lives than infants provide.

The Ultimate Question for Late-Timing Mothers: An Only Child?

Several late-timing mothers remarked that the issue of whether or not to have a second child was a troubling one for them and their husbands, especially when they considered how old they might be when a second child is born. One mother, who was 35 when her first child was born, said:

I think the most difficult thing about having a child at this age for me (and the advantages far outweigh the disadvantages) is realizing that there is even a more important question than having any children—it is whether you want to have only one child. . . . There is something about having an only child that, when you're older, becomes a panicky kind of decision. I mean that's a decision you have to make. Having children is generally not a decision—you're lucky to have them—but the idea of having an only child is a real decision. I just made a comment this morning that I'm definitely going to have a child in the next couple of years. But when I'm forty I'm definitely not going to have another child. I'm thinking about the irony of that entire statement—of course you can have a child after forty, but I might be menopausal after forty.

Another late-timing mother expressed her concern regarding other people's attitudes:

People's attitudes generally indicate that it makes sense to have two children. This is the feeling that I get. People feel that two is OK, but if you have three and you're going into your forties you must really be nuts. I find that if I even mention that we're considering having another child, people just look at me as though I've lost my mind. That's been a consideration for me. I keep thinking that I shouldn't be deciding this on the basis of what other people think. I found that it has made a difference to me and I keep thinking, "Is that really crazy?"

It is clear that having a second child is an issue with which many late-timers struggle.

Summary

Early-timing mothers more often mentioned being connected to their children and families, physically caring for their children, and being needed and loved by their children as the most pleasurable experiences for them. During a group discussion, a 24-year-old mother of two small children said, with much feeling:

I like someone to hug all the time—I'm not a real demonstrative person, but with my children I can be and it's comfortable for me—I enjoy that. They get to the point where they don't want to do that anymore—that makes me sad.

In general, early-timing mothers seem most comfortable "being" with their children. As one of these mothers said:

I find the happiest moments when Jimmy and Susan are sitting with me and they're contented and they're just with me.

Early-timing mothers seem genuinely to enjoy playing on the floor with their children:

> I just think this [mothering] is the neatest time in my whole life. I had a career before this, and I would just as soon give that up and stay home and be with these kids and play on the floor.

Because of this preference for merging and connecting with their children, these mothers particularly enjoy the early period of parenthood, when there is more of a symbiotic relationship between mother and child. During later infancy and toddlerhood, however, when the child begins to separate from the mother and to assert his or her own individual characteristics, these mothers may experience more anxiety. The tensions of parenthood for early-timing mothers may mirror their concurrent struggle with separation/ individuation in their own adult lives.

Late-timing mothers seem more comfortable "doing" things with their children. They enjoy focusing on and encouraging verbal rather than non-verbal communication, teaching children new skills, and watching them grow and develop. All of these processes involve more distance in the mother–child relationship. When asked what was most pleasurable for her, one late-timing mother said:

> I'm happiest going places or doing things (even doing tasks) in a leisurely fashion with my husband and baby.

Other late-timers stated their pleasure in watching their children's growth and development. These responses point to the possibility that the late-timing mother may have a greater capacity to experience her child's growth and development as a gain rather than a loss for her within the mother–child relationship. Furthermore, because of her personality style, her education, and her stage of life, the late-timer may be more reflective and appreciative of her child's new-found cognitive skills and ability to communicate verbally with her.

Other findings indicate that these women are also extremely comfortable with the early stages of their children's lives. They reported pleasure in experiencing physical and emotional closeness with their baby—in holding and nursing the child. Most of the late-timers found nurturing their infants extremely pleasurable and satisfying. Yet many late-timers also reported that the early months were difficult times because they felt uncomfortable having someone so dependent on them and because they were not receiving the immediate verbal feedback to which they had been accustomed in their careers. Furthermore, they deeply resent the loss of personal freedom that goes along with motherhood. These women need personal space and secure it for themselves. The tensions of parenthood for late-timing mothers may reflect the struggle with intimacy and affiliation in their own adult lives, as many of these women are just beginning to explore this aspect of their personality. (This issue is explored more fully in chapter 9.)

4

Motherhood: A Balancing Act

THERE is literature that suggests that if a woman has her first baby later in adulthood, she might not be an adequate mother. One author has claimed that if a woman develops her autonomous self through a career in her twenties, she will later have difficulty opening herself up enough to allow a child to connect with her.[1] This connecting with the child is a necessary process, because the infant needs to be strengthened by the emotional support the mother is able to give when she is totally aware of and with the child—in both an emotional and a physical sense. D.W. Winnicott refers to this support as the "holding environment."[2]

Much of the traditional literature seems to stress that to provide this type of environment, all of the mother's energy must be focused in one direction. Deutsch and others have indicated that for girls who plan for a profession and a family, there is a deep and powerful competition for emotional energy that cannot serve one goal without being drawn away from the other.[3] The implication seems to be that if a mother has been or is actively involved with interests of her own (such as a career or work outside the home), she will have great difficulty creating an appropriate postnatal environment in which the infant and mother are "properly" connected.

Jessner and her colleagues have provided a more optimistic resolution of the conflict engendered by a dual focus on career and motherhood. These researchers reported on observations of psychiatric residents who are mothers. They found that, though these women struggled with divided devotion, this compromise afforded them an opportunity to experience themselves as whole persons and to enjoy their children without burdening them with resentment or "expecting them to compensate for sacrifice."[4] Baruch, Barnett, and Rivers recently demonstrated that "doing or achieving are at least as important to the lives of women as are relationships and feelings." In their study, women who attained a high "well-being" score attended to both "mastery" (the doing and achieving aspects of life) and "pleasure" (the relationship/feeling aspect of life).[5] The findings from my study support this more optimistic view.

As chapter 3 suggested, late-timing mothers who were more career-oriented, both prenatally and postnatally, expressed more comfort than the early-timing mothers with the autonomous aspects of motherhood. These aspects include setting appropriate limits and providing adequate discipline, watching the child grow and develop, and separating physically from the child. However, these same mothers were also comfortable with the aspects of parenthood that involve more physical and emotional intimacy with their children, such as nursing and the children's dependency on them.

Although late-timers consider it important that their children be verbal, independent, and exploring, they also expressed much pleasure with being physically and emotionally close to their children. They reported little more difficulty in establishing an appropriate postnatal environment than did the more traditional mothers, who timed the birth of their first children during their twenties.

Ideally, in the early months, the mother allows the infant to be totally connected and merged. Several theorists have stressed the importance of the mother's capacity to enjoy the narcissistic state of pregnancy and early motherhood—that is, to enjoy and give in to the dependency of the child on the mother and, in a sense, the dependency of the mother on the child.[6] According to Benedek, the mother's need for closeness with the baby is as strong as the infant's need for the "mother's warmth, tenderness and care of him." Benedek has spoken of this as a "normal symbiotic process between mother and child . . . as it enables the mother to encompass the growing child in her personality."[7] Winnicott has discussed the need to "give in to mothering," and Lichtenstein has stressed the capacity for the mother to "pleasure in mothering"[8]—an important factor in the healthy development of both mother and child. For Benedek, the experience of mothering requires the mother to express "passive receptive tendencies," which allow the appropriate emotional energy to be stored and used "for the sake of the child."[9]

However, Benedek has pointed out that although women's ideals are easily integrated in simple societies, this is not so true in our own culture. Our society conveys to the woman the active, achievement-oriented, extroverted, and, in some sense, "masculine" ideal of our civilization. For Benedek, this ideal is in conflict with the passive tendencies inherent in the mothering role. Benedek has claimed that many mothers who are deeply affected by our cultural emphasis on this achievement goal cannot permit themselves to become passive and dependent. Instead, these mothers repress their dependent needs and overcompensate for them, sometimes to the point of exhaustion. Sometimes, when mothering becomes a continual task after the child is born, "these women suffer from guilt reactions if they sense any deviation from the required standards of motherliness."[10] Both of these reactions deplete the "source of motherliness" and make "nurturing the child and satisfaction of one's needs difficult."[11]

In a longitudinal study focusing on experienced mothers' adaptation to pregnancy and the first year of life, the quality of mothering was negatively correlated with the reported "degree of self masculinity and a more egalitarian style."[12] These researchers suggested the possibility that "more feminine and more traditional women," who exhibit the "required selflessness and relative lack of differentiation," more closely approach the cultural stereotype of "good mothering" than do the more "masculine women" and women who have "negotiated more egalitarian marriages."[13]

Theodore Lidz concurred that women who achieve autonomy in forming careers must establish "very firm boundaries," which are difficult to "relax" sufficiently when the woman later becomes a mother. This is so because, as a mother, a woman must form a "symbiotic union" with her infant so that the infant can become sufficiently dependent on her.[14] These conclusions support Benedek's views regarding the need for the mother to feel comfortable with the regression and dependency evoked by pregnancy and infancy and the likelihood that certain types of women might have more difficulty dealing with this regression and dependency.

In my study, the late-timing mothers were women who had invested their early adulthood (their twenties) in work outside the home. These women had created an identity based on their own accomplishments and had defined it on their own terms. They appear similar to the women that Benedek, Grossman, and Lidz referred to as "women with other interests"—women who have been more affected by the achievement-oriented focus of our culture. These late-timers are women who several theorists predicted would have difficulty with the necessary passive tendencies inherent in being a mother.

The findings from my study indicate that women who timed the birth of their first children early in adulthood perceive themselves as more submissive and less achievement-oriented. Furthermore, they have defined themselves in terms of their relationships with their children and husbands. These early-timing mothers are similar to the more "traditional" women defined in the literature.

The results of my study seem to conflict with several theoretical formulations regarding women who are more career- or achievement-oriented and how they tend to cope with mothering a child. Within this study, late-timing mothers, though experiencing some discomfort in meeting the intense dependency needs of their infants during the early months, were also delighted about caring for their infants. These mothers appeared to be highly invested in their mothering role during the early months of their children's lives. In fact, as will be demonstrated in chapter 7, many of them did not want to return to careers and jobs that they had once enjoyed and that had held their attention and focus for several years before motherhood.

As one late-timing mother said during a group discussion when asked what was most pleasurable for her about motherhood:

> I wanted a baby—I get such a tremendous pleasure out of being able to pour all of this love and affection into Sarah.

Another mother, whose first child was born when she was 33 years of age, said, "I like the physical closeness." In many ways, the late-timing mother appeared to be energized, not depleted, by her role as a mother. One mother, who was working a few hours per week and who had her first child at 31 years of age, reported:

> What I loved about Michael was that even before he came into the world—babies generate a lot of love—I got a lot of love. When Michael came out, he got a lot of love—it just loosened up the atmosphere—babies are great for that. The other thing is—it takes you out of yourself. I think I've become a lot less selfish—more loving, relaxed, and easygoing. I'm not concentrating so much on myself. I have a lot more energy.

Furthermore, if good mothering is defined as the capacity to cope with the oscillations between holding on to and letting go of the child, the late-timing mother may more closely resemble the ideal mother. In my study, the late-timing mothers more frequently evidenced comfort with two different aspects of parenting—the capacity for connecting and being close to their children and the ability to separate from their children. The early-timing mothers more frequently reported satisfaction with only the earliest phases of the child's life—when the children were "lap babies" and required a more symbiotic tie with the mother.

These younger women appear to enjoy living out the "fantasy of symbiotic union" that Mahler refers to—they enjoy that early bodily tie. However, these same mothers express discomfort and difficulty when the child needs to begin to separate and individuate from the mother. Indeed, these mothers are less comfortable than the late-timing mothers with the child's increasing verbal skills and general growth and development. As one early-timing mother indicated:

> My four-year-old is now really expressing his personality—we get into this clash—as long as they can't verbalize I'm fine, but once they start, this is difficult for me.

This is in direct contrast to late-timing mothers, who reported that the most pleasurable experiences for them were when their children began to verbalize and communicate, as illustrated by the following comment:

> Right now—with a four-year-old—to be able to discuss things—to tell him something and have him respond and ask questions.

The theme of many comments by late-timing mothers was "I love watching my child grow and develop." The following excerpt from a small-group discussion with eight late-timing mothers beautifully illustrates this theme as well as how much these late-timing mothers enjoy motherhood.

A 40-year-old graduate student with one child: I wish I could remember who had said this—we went to a huge bash at the library and some grande dame who had worked with Marie Montesorri was there and saw Sarah in the backpack and said, "There is nothing so wonderful as to watch the opening of the mind." Somehow that just really caught what I'm doing with my parenting—which is to sit and see how she develops. All of us have vignettes about how your child views the world—they start out in the world as a curled up seven-pound thing and turn into this gigantic powerful human being. It's very exciting to see it happen.

A 37-year-old mother of two preschoolers: That's what I feel. Sometimes the times when I most appreciate are when I'm kind of sitting back and watching David from a distance—it's amazing and incredible to watch.

A mother who works at home as a typist and has four children under age 5—including 9-month old twins: Those are my most pleasurable moments too—the development—watching the development because I could just turn on when I hear Jeremy look at me and say, "I love you Mommy"— after he has already done something. I really get pleasure out of just watching them—pulling each other around by barrettes. There is something in every-thing they do. There are times when I'm ready to pull all my hairs out, but in the next five minutes it's what they say to me next. I can't complain because I really enjoy watching them and seeing them explore things—things that maybe I don't even want to see them do. I could write a book on the things my chil-dren have gotten into. It's really fun to talk about it—the pleasure is there just watching and thinking "what was it like."

A 38-year-old mother of two: I think that's why I'm at home, because I don't want someone else to see these things—getting the chance to see what's happening with my children. You do have to make a decision. I have several friends that have made that decision regarding whether or not to stay at home. I have one friend who really likes working. She loves her child but she likes to do her work and sees her child in the evening. But I really feel that they are not young very long and I hate to miss out on all these changes. It is fascinating and even more so because they're my own children.

These mothers learn and develop less *with* their children (as early-timing mothers do) than at a distance from them, while observing them.

Although late-timing mothers are involved with their children, there is enough distance and sense of separateness (from both their own parents and their children) that the experience of mothering provides a "reliving of an experience," rather than a feeling of "living through" the child's life, which was often observed in the responses of early-timing mothers. It is difficult to see the world through a child's eyes without having achieved a certain dis-tance and without having achieved a certain level of individuation. As one late-timing mother said:

One thing that gives me an enormous amount of pleasure is being able to relive my own childhood experiences—seeing the world again through the eyes of a child. I think that that has really been exciting for me, and hopefully it's made me a little bit of a better person as a result.

Late-timers have less of a tendency to live their lives through their children because they are less dependent on their children as a source of their own self-esteem and identity. As noted earlier, early-timing mothers often view their children as extensions of themselves.

Because late-timers are able to secure the necessary personal space for themselves within the mother–child relationship, they may find it more comfortable to set appropriate boundaries between themselves and their children. These boundaries may enable the late-timers to move in and out of the physically and emotionally close relationship with their children as the children's demands change over time. This capacity may explain why late-timing mothers seem better able to balance connecting with and letting go of their children. This pattern may contribute to some of the differences we observed between early- and late-timing mothers in regard to meeting their own needs and those of their children—the focus of the next chapter.

5

A Mother's Dilemma:
Meeting Her Own and
Her Child's Needs

A s discussed earlier, motherhood has its share of both gratifications and frustrations. It is evident that there are inherent tensions for a woman in her role as a mother. Especially during the preschool years of a child's life, a mother must cope with the competing emotional needs of her young child and herself. In a recent article by a colleague and myself, we stated:

A woman must learn to balance her own needs and identity as a person with the child's need for appropriate merging and distancing. The child's own developmental push requires a constant shifting in the mother's balance between herself and her child.[1]

Research on Female Development

Current researchers in the area of female adult development have been critical of theory that has been generated for all adults but is based solely on studies of the lives of men. Adult development, as described by Daniel Levinson and his colleagues[2] and by George Valliant,[3] has been defined too closely in terms of the importance of autonomy and individuation, neglecting the importance of relationships and connectedness with others. Traditional theories of adult development have focused on the development of self and work and have not stressed the importance of significant relationships—such as those with spouses, children, and friends. Yet this network of relationships is often the very fabric of women's lives.

Carol Gilligan's criticism of the traditional perspective on adult development has been that this view equates maturity with personal autonomy and describes attachments to others as developmental impediments.[4] Women's development has been measured against a male standard of separation as the process leading toward the formation of identity. Gilligan has claimed that a crucial shortcoming in adult development research has been the failure to recognize the importance of relationships and connection to others, leading toward a "maturity of interdependence."[5] Many female researchers who have studied women's lives agree that, for women, the tasks of identity and attachment seem fused.[6]

Differences during early childhood development set the stage for contrasts in how men and women develop during adolescence and adulthood. A woman's sense of gender identity develops from her connection, attachment, and identification with her female model—in most cases, her mother. A girl tends to emerge from this early period with a "basis for empathy built into her primary definition of self in a way that boys do not."[7] A woman "experiences herself always as more continuous with another" and has a tendency to fuse or merge with others. For men, who must separate from mother and identify with father, separation and individuation become the focus of gender identity. Men tend to "separate self from other."[8] Thus, whereas boys describe themselves as distinct by locating their particular position within the world—defining themselves through separation from others—the feminine self develops as it is experienced through relationships with others. In Carol Gilligan's study of abortion, she discovered that female subjects defined their identity in terms of relationship with others and made moral judgments according to a standard of responsibility for the person involved, rather than a standard of moral rights. Girls thus tend to describe and define themselves through actions that bring them into connection with others; their identity is defined in a context of relationship and is judged by a standard of responsibility and care. As Gilligan has noted: "Women bring to the life cycle a different point of view and order human experiences in terms of different priorities."[9]

Many researchers have indicated that, for women, affiliative needs are primary and are valued as much as or more than self-enhancement.[10] However, women have been deflected away from pleasing themselves, because they value affiliation and concern so highly. Jean Baker Miller points out that "acting for oneself is made to seem like depriving others or hurting them."[11] Because of the dominant role that afilliations have played in their lives, many women cannot allow themselves to feel that their life activities are carried out for themselves. This is particularly true for mothers of preschool children, who are especially called to a state of "selflessness" and giving to another person.

The main dilemma for mothers is to remain nurturing without sacrificing themselves in the process. The emotional stress of mothering comes from the feelings aroused by the intense relationship with the small child; for a long time, the needs of the child take priority over the mother's own needs.[12] Thus, it can be difficult to be in a nurturing role without being exploited. Elaine Heffner has claimed:

> For a mother to interact with her child successfully on the basis of the child's needs and her own requires the capacity for independent observation and judgment. In other words, she herself must be able to function autonomously.[13]

Thus, autonomy and independent judgment are needed as much for mothering as they are in the professional world.

Female development can be contrasted to male development in that women have a tendency to place the care and responsibility of others ahead of their own needs and concerns. The responses of women interviewed in this study corroborate the importance of connection and relationship with others in women's lives. They substantiate, as well, the difficulty most women experience, when involved in a close relationship with another person, in relating to their own needs. For both early- and late-timing mothers, the dilemma of coping with the self–other tension presents a challenge. This challenge is illustrated by a poignant statement by a late-timing mother of a 6-month-old daughter:

> I spend far too much time with my child. I need more breaks so I can pursue other goals. Right now I can't afford paid child care until I start earning more money—so my breaks are limited when I can't get my husband and friends to help with child care. I'm reluctant to get a part-time job with an agency because I want to develop my private practice and because my baby still wakes a lot at night and I'm exhausted a lot. So, I feel life is a Catch 22 at present!

Early-Timing Mothers Perceive Meeting Emotional Needs as a Zero-Sum Game

The loss of personal freedom, time, and space was a common theme cited by both early- and late-timing mothers as the most difficult aspect of parenthood. However, this theme was more frequently expressed by late-timers in response to a variety of questions throughout both phases of data collection.

Furthermore, although both groups indicated the importance of having "time for yourself," late-timing mothers are more able to act upon this need, and they do find time for themselves.

Early-timing mothers expressed more conflict about meeting their own needs. Several young women indicated that the loss of personal time and sense of identity was very difficult for them; yet they do not or cannot act in ways that would ensure that some of this time and sense of well being could be restored. Early-timers do not see the need to "feed and nurture" themselves, as do many of the late-timing mothers. One young mother stated:

> I'd like to start that off [discussing what is most difficult about motherhood], because the thing that I always came back to on the questionnaire—the thing that I miss most about being a mother—is not having any time to myself. It's a twenty-four-hour-a-day job, and there is no escaping it once you have children. . . . My husband and I don't have any time together, and I don't have any time for myself anymore. That's been the biggest change for me—I guess every mother would probably say that.

Another young mother, who has three children, expressed her confusion about meeting her needs as well as those of others:

> I just wish I could get to feel very satisfied of how much time I spend with them, so that it feels good enough. I feel that I do a lot with them. I'm home with them—but I'm never satisfied; yet at the same time I feel that I'm putting myself last. I'm not bitter but I feel, and Elaine [another group member] agreed, yes, neglected—I'm neglecting myself at the same time.

In general, early-timers appeared to be less aware of themselves as separate people apart from their children and had more difficulty clarifying their own needs as separate from those of their children. Perhaps because these young women are less able to recognize their own emotional needs, they are less able to elicit help from their husbands when they experience frustration as mothers. (This issue is explored further in chapter 6). Furthermore, early-timers may encourage their children and husbands to be dependent on them, because being needed by others is the main source of their self-esteem. Two young mothers, who were 22 and 23, respectively, when their first children were born, commented:

> Freedom is my main problem—not finding any kind of time. In the beginning my husband was afraid of the kids—he didn't know what to do with them. He

would walk in the door and I would be like—"You take them"—and he would say, "But what do you do?"

My husband works nights—he comes home and I say, "Here, take her—I'm going to take a bath. And he says, "Well, I worked all day," and I say "Well, what do you think I did?" He says, "Well, you sat home all day." The issue of freedom—there just isn't any.

One 26-year-old mother of two discussed her conflict over meeting her own needs in this blatant confession to the group:

I've been very selfless for a while—it's just the kids. But I'll make a confession. Today, with one son stopping up the toilet and cutting his hair and my other son lying to me—when I was out at the store I hadn't taken time to feed myself—I had one dollar left and there was a pizza stand. I went up and said "Kids, you can't have any, you don't deserve it—I'm having myself a bit of pizza." I had never done that before. They kept standing there waiting, expecting me to give them some, and I didn't. It took six years to be able to do it, and it felt like fun. I'm sure that if they had been good today I would have gotten one slice and cut it in half and given it to them and I still would have been hungry.

For early-timing mothers, meeting needs seems more of a zero-sum game, in which the child is losing out if the mother meets her own needs. Late-timing mothers recognize that if a mother "feeds and nourishes" herself emotionally, she has more to give to the child. One late-timer poignantly stated the most difficult aspect about motherhood for her:

Having to put somebody else's needs before my own—even being married, when we were both working, things were on a more even keel. I loved nursing, yet I had to quit when I was tired—I had to relax. When I'm on the phone and she needs me, I just want to finish a conversation. You need to be nourished because you give and give—sometimes I forget to receive support and nourishment—then you feel starved.

In the following comments, two late-timing mothers discuss the importance of "tuning in" to their own needs:

A 35-year-old mother of 3-year-old twin boys: I thought I would be so ideal as a parent and that I wouldn't mind all the self-sacrifice. It's easy for me to put my needs first. I'm willing to do that. I have a good babysitter—I use her a lot.

The twins are doing fine—they don't need me all the time. I just never thought I would so easily give in to my own needs. If I want to read for five more minutes, I do it. I'm a lot happier.

A 38-year-old mother of two preschoolers: That's true for me, too. It says something regarding late-timing mothers. The first year, we go through reading all the books—we all talked to the child since infancy—the books say to do that. Our own kids talk a lot. We read a lot and then we react on a gut level. I learned I had to take time for myself. My husband travels a lot—he's very supportive when he's around. I need two hours a day in the late afternoon—it's called "arsenic hour." I have a sitter come and I read by myself. If I was younger, I probably wouldn't have gotten a sitter.

Statistical analyses of the questionnaire data and the group discussion data corroborate these differences between early- and late-timing mothers regarding meeting the needs of others—their children and their husbands—and meeting their own needs (see table 5 in the appendix).

Late-Timing Mothers Consider Organization and Planning the Keys to Meeting Emotional Needs

It is significant that late-timing mothers seem to have found ways to handle these pressures more successfully than early-timing mothers, who, even if aware of the dilemma, are unable to extricate themselves from it. As mentioned earlier, the late-timing mothers used structure and organization within the home and/or a paid job or other interest or activity to help them cope with balancing their own needs and those of their children. One 36-year-old mother commented:

You have to organize—you have to set aside time for yourself. It's very easy to say "I don't have time for myself," but I think that . . . you have to make time for yourself—there are things that you have to put away. I find myself saying I have to do this for me or somehow something in the house is going to get thrown under the carpet for a while—not the children—the importance of time management.

Another late-timing mother, who has two young sons, has decided not to return to her profession until the children are older. She reported that following the birth of her second child, it was easier to meet some of her own needs.

I will wait with Jacob [her second child] to see how much he really needs me. If I hear him crying after I put him in for a nap, I won't go running. I'll wait to see if he's really serious about it, and of course if he's panicking, I'll go to him. It seems to have worked. . . . And also, I feel less guilty—I will leave Jacob in the Swingomatic in front of *Sesame Street* to take a shower.

One late-timing mother, who has a 2-year-old daughter and is pregnant, has retired from her position as a physical therapist. This woman has found that writing a daily journal has helped her balance her own needs and those of her children:

I found something I enjoy doing is writing—keeping a journal works for me— this may develop into something. I have a filing cabinet which my husband bought for me. If I don't do enough of it, I really suffer—it is so fulfilling for me. I'm writing for a newsletter now—trying to do it is crazy at times.

Late-Timers Learned to Make It on Their Own Before Motherhood

Women who delayed childbearing learned how to care for themselves well before they became mothers. This stands them in good stead when they are trying to balance their own needs and those of their children. One 35-year-old mother of two preschool children said:

Needs are all in what you make them. . . . A person has to start taking care of themselves whether they need it or not—they have to feed themselves as much as their child has eaten.

In my discussions with the mothers, I found that these late-timers had developed a sense of identity before motherhood. They had learned to take care of themselves, and they had learned to enjoy being alone. During one group discussion, late-timing mothers revealed the importance of having "lived on their own" during their twenties, when they learned to take care of themselves and to survive on their own. One mother of two preschoolers said:

I had to deal with this fear of being by myself—I had roommates—but then one year I didn't—I forced myself not to have any. Not physical fear, but a fear of . . . being alone. . . . I'd gone to boarding school—I'd gone to college—there were a lot of kids in my family—I'd never been by myself, and I think that's what happened. I don't think I could have gotten married until I dealt with that.

Most of the group agreed that they had had similar experiences in their twenties. The following is an excerpt from this group discussion:

It's a lot to go out and earn your own living and support yourself and pay your own rent.

To occupy yourself and sit by yourself.

And be sick by yourself.

If you can get through that, then you really know that you can make it.

I think that the part of my experience that has formed my identity is that I know now that no matter what happens I'd be OK.

Something to fall back on—if you've coped with it all up until now—you'll be OK.

It may be painful or terrible, but I can do it and there isn't that uncertainty about myself.

I got married right out of college, but then my husband died about seven years later. [There were no children from this marriage.] Then I was on my own for a few years and then remarried. I had it both ways, and although I'd never want to go through the experience of having someone die, I have to admit that during that time I went back to school and did additional traveling. It was good—looking back, I really grew in the number of years I was supposed to be by myself—I can see it from both ends and I'm better off in having married late the second time and having had a chance to find out who I am.

I think it's really hard to figure out an identity when there are other people involved who are really affected by it—like your husband and especially your kids. They're definitely going to be either standing in the way or influencing you. It won't really be just you—it's a group decision. Being somewhat uncertain of my identity to begin with, I was really glad that I had a chance to say "This is me—I know it's me."

One late-timer, who had been married previously during her late teens, discussed the difference between her sense of self at that point and how she experiences herself now as a result of her struggle in her twenties:

I tried real, real hard not to be alone—not to grow up. I got married when I was nineteen—the marriage didn't last very long—it was a real disaster. I bought the dream—we were going to have kids right away [as it turned out, they did not have children]—I wasn't going to work. I came from a pretty traditional family, and I didn't have any role models for working and being independent. When my marriage blew up in my face, I had to take a real hard look at myself. When I think about that experience, I think that there are probably easier ways to grow up, but I'm really glad that this experience happened to me, or otherwise I would have been a real vegetable.

Early-Timing Mothers and Identity Foreclosure

Women who have timed the birth of their first children during their late teens or early twenties have spent those years focusing on marriage and children. They have not had the experience of learning to count on themselves before taking care of children and a home. To some extent, these younger mothers may have suffered from identity foreclosure—becoming very enmeshed with a husband and child before discovering who they are as adults in their own right. Identity foreclosure is one resolution of the crisis of later adolescence. This resolution involves a "series of premature decisions about one's identity, often in response to the demands of others."[14] A person who forecloses on her identity has not had ample time to experiment with various roles, try alternatives, and choose those that fit a pattern that feels right for her. Work on identity issues is a focus of the late adolescent and the young adult in his or her early twenties. Women who bear their first children during this period develop an identity that has a more reflective tone—a sense of self that is more dependent on relationships with others.

Findings from the small-group discussions and from the questionnaire indicate that late-timers have learned to count on themselves, whereas early-timers have been more dependent on others for emotional gratification. The raters commented that late-timing mothers discovered pleasure and relaxation in spending time alone (reading, studying, working on a project) as well as pleasure in being with others (socializing, friendships, and so on). Early-timing mothers rarely derived pleasure from spending time by themselves.

On the questionnaire, when asked to describe her "happiest moment during the week," a typical response from an early-timing mother was, "When the three of us do something together" or "Cuddling, rolling on the floor with my baby and husband." A typical response from a late-timing mother was either a self-oriented activity, such as "When I enjoy some time to myself after a long day" or "Any time I can devote to myself—reading or writing," or a response indicating pleasure in activities with others as well as pleasure in activities pursued alone. Comments from two late-timing mothers illustrate the latter type of response:

> When my husband and I get a chance to talk. Watching my husband play with our daughter. Doing something with my daughter we both enjoy. Spending time alone. Completing a task.

> Evenings after supper when we're all full and relaxing; weekends when I can relax with no rigid schedule and enjoy my daughter; times alone for study in my library.

These findings suggest that late-timers enjoy spending time by themselves and feel enriched and refreshed by this ability to nourish themselves. This ability to enjoy time alone may enable these mothers to "feed" themselves emotionally. Early-timers do not derive the same comfort from being alone and need the connection with others to experience pleasure.

Women who delay childbearing are spending those years of postponement learning how to make a living and are moving more toward autonomous functioning. Other research on women's lives has concluded that women who delay childbearing are "better equipped to take care of themselves" and that with the increasing rate of divorce, women may be making sure that they can manage on their own before taking on the "increased responsibility of motherhood."[15] Furthermore, Baruch and her colleagues found that women in their thirties felt better about themselves, had higher self-esteem, and were able to see that their own needs were met. The women in their study typically reported that "it was in their twenties, not at midlife, that they felt the most uncertain of their worth, the least pleased with themselves."[16]

It would seem that younger women might have more difficulty identifying their own needs and taking care of themselves. Because late-timing mothers learned how to take care of themselves well before they became mothers, they are better able to balance their own needs and those of their children—the dual tasks of motherhood.

Satisfaction with Parenthood

The ability of the late-timing mother to meet her own needs as well as those of her children may help explain some unexpected results obtained from the women's rankings on the questionnaire regarding their satisfaction with various aspects of their lives. These aspects included their relationship with their husband, their relationship with their children, their activities other than paid work (cooking, gardening, sewing, and so forth), paid work, their relationships with friends and relatives, and unpaid activities with others (volunteer work, clubs, and the like).

The women were asked to consider their lives as a whole and to rank these various activities in order of the degree of satisfaction derived from them during the past month (see table 6). Statistical analysis indicated that early- and late-timing mothers differed significantly in their rankings of only one activity—"Relationship(s) with child/children." Late-timing mothers more frequently ranked it number one, claiming that relationships with their children provide them with the most satisfaction among all the activities. Twenty-two of the late-timing mothers (56.4 percent) ranked children as number one, whereas only fourteen of the early-timing mothers (36 percent) ranked children as number one.

To determine whether working outside the home made a difference in the respondents' rankings on this question, I closely examined the occupations of the late-timing mothers who ranked relationships with children as number one.[17] Whether or not a late-timing mother is employed outside the home does not seem to affect the level of satisfaction she experiences in relating to her children.

Furthermore, an examination of how mothers spend their time disclosed the very significant finding that although the late-timers spent only about half as much time with their children as the early-timing mothers did, they appeared to be much more satisfied with this aspect of their lives. On the questionnaire, the women were asked to estimate the number of hours during an ordinary week that they devoted to various activities (see table 7).[18] One of the two activities in which early- and late-timing mothers differed statistically (regarding number of hours spent during a week) was "Time spent with children other than tasks." Although both groups of mothers spend more time with their children than in any other activity, early-timers spent significantly more time (twice as much) with their children in nontask activities than late-timers did.

Because I recognized that a greater number of late-timing mothers were employed outside the home—and that this variable could be contributing to the difference in variance—time spent with children and hours worked (for both groups of early- and late-timing mothers) were subjected to an analysis of covariance technique.[19] The results were essentially the same.

Although early- and late-timing mothers appeared to be equally satisfied with the timing of the birth of their first children, late-timing mothers scored significantly higher when ranking their children as providing the greatest source of satisfaction within their lives—even though they were spending only about half as much time with their children as early-timing mothers. This result seems to support the growing evidence from this study that women who have other interests—that is, who spend time meeting some of their own needs—derive a greater degree of satisfaction from their role as a mother.

Perhaps children have greater meaning for women who have delayed childbirth and who have given up important careers to remain at home with their children. On the other hand, because their children provide them with the greatest source of satisfaction, these mothers may place added pressures on their children to perform at a much higher level. This may be especially true when we consider that women who delay childbirth tend to be very goal- and achievement-oriented. As one late-timer remarked:

Having a child is like a planned project. What if it doesn't turn out right?

Another late-timer, referring to herself and other late-timing mothers she knew, commented: "There's a terrible tendency for us to raise children who are on the way to Yale." This high degree of expectation placed on the child may or may not be appropriate, depending on the child and his or her parents. This tendency to pressure the child to provide satisfaction in the mother's life may, in fact, increase the tension within the mother–child relationship. Further longitudinal research examining the direct effects of the timing of parenthood on children throughout various developmental stages may help us understand these tentative results.

Summary

A major issue for the human community may be the "question of how to create a way of life that includes serving others without being subservient."[20] In their study of women's lives, Baruch and her colleagues found that a woman who feels good about herself and her life, and who "is able to see that her own needs are met as well as those of others is more able to relate to others in a healthy way."[21]

The late-timing mothers who participated in my study seemed most capable of coping with this self–other dilemma. This ability to balance their own emotional demands and those of others may contribute to the degree of satisfaction these late-timers experienced in their relationship with their children.

6

A Mother's Support System: Friends, Parents, and Husband

The Importance of Support Systems

Everyone needs some sort of support network to function effectively in society. Social support reinforces people's belief that they are cared for and loved in mutual relationships and enhances their ability to cope with crisis and change. Social support also provides the family unit with the strength to cope with changes throughout the life cycle.

It is believed that a family's vulnerability to stress relates to the degree to which the family is connected or unconnected to the community. The amount of support, feedback, and sense of congruence with its community may determine the level of the family's adaptive interaction.[1] Thus, a family that functions well may do so because its members receive a great deal of support from forces outside the family.

Families in the perinatal and postnatal period of family development have a special need for outside support, because this is one of the most stressful times in the human life cycle. Studies indicate a relationship between adequate social supports and optimal functioning during this stressful time.[2] As the preceding chapter indicated, mothers of preschool children are coping with stress and transition whether or not they are working outside the home. During the group discussions and on the questionnaire responses, both early- and late-timing mothers stated their need for outside emotional support to function in their role.

When women were asked to share how they cope with the struggle of handling their child's needs and their own needs, one 26-year-old mother with two preschool children said:

> I think the biggest thing is support—if you have support from your husband and from friends who have children the same age, you can do anything. I have

a couple of close friends who have children—thank God! You need outside contacts—not only for yourself but for your children. It's so important to be able to socialize with your peers.

The following excerpt from a small-group discussion with eight late-timing mothers relates to the issue of what helps them cope with the tensions of parenthood—particularly, how they survived that first year with a child:

> For me—you had a question on the questionnaire about support—I put the support of friends right on top.

> I think so too.

> Having the twins—you don't realize the support. I didn't cook a meal for almost four weeks. You don't realize the support of your neighbors and friends. One of my friends took my older child to the library every week.

> When you have that first child, you have to establish a whole network of friends.

Although both early- and late-timing mothers acknowledged the need for outside support, the two groups differed in how they take care of this need. Patterns that emerged from the statistical analysis of the data suggest that whereas late-timers rely more on the emotional support of friends during the early years of parenting ($p < .01$), early-timers rely more on relationships with extended family, other than husband and parents ($p < .02$). In fact, almost twice as many late-timing mothers as early-timing mothers (52 percent versus 28 percent) indicated that friends and neighbors provided the greatest degree of emotional support during the early years of parenthood. These results were supported by comments from the women; early-timing mothers frequently mentioned relationships with sisters and aunts as helpful to them. Moreover, early-timers are more enmeshed in relationships with immediate and extended family members and do not reach out to friends and neighbors as often as late-timers do.

Friendships are Important to Late-Timing Mothers

During the pilot study, the importance of support systems and friendship patterns emerged as extremely critical to the daily functioning of late-timing mothers. I decided to explore this issue in greater depth, because I wondered whether there were differences in how early- and late-timing mothers related to support systems and friendship groups. Therefore, during the formal research study, I asked participants to rate the importance of friendships during their career as mothers. I also asked the women to rate the degree of difficulty they experienced in asking for help and the source of emotional support they received (if any) during the early years of parenting.

From these data, there was strong evidence that during the years in which these women are parenting small children, friendships seem more important to late-timing than to early-timing mothers. This statement was supported by results from the questionnaire ($p < .06$) and by clinical impressions from the small-group discussions. Both data sources revealed that late-timing mothers need and cherish relationships with friends during the early years of parenting.

The feeling of isolation that is common among women who delay childbirth may help explain the evidence suggesting that late-timers reach out more to develop friendship networks during the early years of parenting. Because there are no readily available support systems, late-timers must work at creating them. Late-timing mothers often do not have the close support of extended family, who frequently are geographically distant from them and from whom the late-timers are more emotionally separated. Late-timing mothers may also experience a sense of isolation within their neighborhoods, because the families living nearby are often early-timing parents with older children. These early-timers are in a different stage of parenthood and have less in common with late-timing parents. The following comments from two late-timing mothers illustrate this sense of isolation.

> I realize that I've had to cut out time with friends. When you're younger, you live in neighborhoods where kids are—everybody's out. When you're older, you don't live where there are row houses with lots of kids. You have to plan your support with play groups. Older parents live in neighborhoods where families have bought their second houses and the kids are babysitting age.

> For me, lack of a support system is a real disadvantage of being an older parent. . . . All my friends went in different directions during the first ten years after college. We will never have neighborhood friends—never have a neighborhood support system—all of our neighbors are older, so their children are older and are doing different things. I can't see myself talking to them on a very personal level. I have children now and no one has them [preschool children] in common with me. Younger parents do things together.

According to a newspaper report, isolation is a common feeling among women who are restructuring their lives as mothers following a career orientation in their twenties and early thirties.[3] One mother, who was working part-time as a lawyer, commented,

> I don't identify with anyone. I don't feel there are any role models.

The late-timers who participated in my study felt isolated for different reasons and were helping to support one another by serving as role models for each other.

One of the implications of these findings is the importance of developing a close supportive network of friends to help with the stresses and the isolation of parenthood. I felt that the late-timing mothers would have become extremely isolated had they not reached out and established an important network or joined an existing support group, such as a parents' group at a nursery school or a nursing mothers' group. This conclusion is illustrated by the following comments from two late-timing mothers who have found help with the strains of motherhood by reaching out to organizations:

> And the difficulty is that unlike any other job, there is nowhere you can go to school. The biggest help for me was the Sheeran School—a parenting center. Here you can find out what the literature says without having a degree in child development. You can get some feeling that you're not a blithering idiot. It's an eight-week thing and then it's once a month forever.

> I really consider nursing mothers to be the greatest. My mother is terrific—I have fantastic in-laws—but with nursing mothers it involves someone I've never met before in my life. We are going to have a relationship where she's going to help me and give me support with nursing. It's a different feeling talking with someone who doesn't know your background and all your problems. She is solely there to listen to you and to help you with your problems. Your mom or somebody else could go into all kinds of things. I found it the best thing to be going for me.

This is not to say that early-timing mothers do not also need support networks or do not experience a sense of isolation in their role as parents, but they did not discuss this issue.

Early-Timing Mothers Rely on Their Mothers and Extended Family

In contrast, the early-timing mothers derived a great deal of emotional support from their own parents. This was clearly illustrated during one group discussion in which several of the women reported that they visit with their mothers on a daily or weekly basis. This was never a pattern among late-timing mothers. This result is not surprising when we consider that early-timing mothers are probably geographically closer and more emotionally connected to extended family than late-timing mothers are. Most of the late-timers are more likely to have parents who are more removed from the child-rearing process than the parents of early-timers, simply because of their ages. This issue will be explored as we examine the women's relationships with their own parents.

Relationships with Parents

Although both groups of mothers relied fairly heavily on their husbands and on their parents for emotional support during the early years of parenting, there were differences in how the two groups perceived their relationships with their parents. Early-timing mothers reported frequent visits with their own parents and/or their in-laws. One young mother, who was 22 when her first child was born, reported how important her relationship with her mother is to her:

> We go almost every weekend to be with my mom and her boyfriend—and stay the weekend. My mom and Don (my husband) don't always see eye to eye, but it must be getting better or we wouldn't continue going. That makes me feel better. I have a good relationship with my mother. I just hope my daughters and me have as good a one as we have when they get older.

Early-timing mothers are much less individuated and are more dependent on their own parents, from whom they still derive a great deal of emotional support. Three other young mothers commented in a similar fashion:

> I see my mother a lot. I'm right around the corner.

> About once a week my sister, my mother, and I make it a point to have lunch together—we rotate houses. . . . It's nice to be with her.

> I'm always on the phone to my mother—every two weeks. Before I moved here, I used to see my mother every day.

These young mothers depend on their mothers, sisters, and female friends for support with child rearing. They have developed a tightly knit support system that seems to work for them. However, these mothers also experience problems in having such close contact with their parents. Their relationships with their parents seem intense but conflicted. The following comments by two young mothers poignantly describe some of this turmoil and conflict:

> Both of our families live in the same town as we do, and there is a problem with that. If you go to them for advice regarding one specific thing, they take that as an open invitation to tell you how to raise your child—both sets of parents have done this. Now that the kids are older I've dealt with it, but I had some rough times when they were little. "Don't let her suck her thumb. Don't let him use a pacifier. Train them by fifteen months." She had a whole different standard for treating her grandchildren than her children—she really mellowed out. The grandchildren would get away with murder compared to what we got away with as kids. It's nice for the kids to see their grandparents regularly, but its hard on the parents.

> My baby is compared to my nieces and nephew constantly. My baby has no teeth, while my nephew has three teeth. She constantly asks "Did he get any teeth yet?" It's almost like a rivalry—I love my nephews and nieces, but I don't want to be jealous of my sister's babies—yet it's almost come to that.

There were no such comments during discussions with late-timing mothers. Late-timers were more wistful about not having regular contact with their parents because of geographical distance. The following excerpt from a group discussion illustrates how late-timers responded when they were asked to discuss whether they had families living in the area and how often they see their parents:

> It's the first time that I've felt that I wished the grandparents lived around the corner, but each of them lives one and one-half hours away. We've always been so grateful before the children came, because it's close enough to visit them but not close enough for drop-ins.

> I think parenthood eminently calls up the need for family and friends—extended family. [Several other mothers agreed.]

> I'd love to have my family closer by.

> Closer—I'd like to be in the same country.

> That's probably something that would keep us in this area—apart from the fact that I like it personally. I think it's nice for my parents and grandmother who are here—to have a young child around. We're lucky to have that—we could

have her as an only child because she has so many cousins with whom she's close.

That was my first babysitting issue. I wanted to leave Laura with somebody who loved her—who I knew I could trust in a very deep way to care for her—in a way that I would care for her. I wanted sisters that I'd never had and aunts and uncles as well.

We came back to this area from Iowa when we knew we were going to have a child. We came home. We were out there without family and without friends and it was crazy. We came home to have a baby.

My family and my husband's family are in the New England area, and we miss them.

Women who time the birth of their first children during their early twenties are still enmeshed with their family of origin, who often live close to them. Women who delay childbirth usually live farther from their families and have developed a more heterogeneous social network to cope with the stresses of parenthood. A typical situation for a late-timer who depends on a supportive network of friends is illustrated by the following comment by a 36-year-old mother of two preschoolers:

My family lives six hours away, and my husband's family is even further away. We see them fairly often, considering the distance. I feel even a greater support from friends—particularly around the baby's birth. We've had wonderful help from friends.

Shifts in Relationships with Parents Following Motherhood

Both early- and late-timing mothers reported shifts in relationships with their own parents as a result of parenthood. Although the early-timers spend a lot of time with their mothers and appear to depend on their parents for emotional support, parenthood also facilitates their emotional separation from their families of origin. Many early-timing mothers reported that having their first children seemed to enhance the cohesion within their nuclear family by helping to break long-established traditions with their own parents. The timing of parenthood in the lives of these younger women is important, in that many of these women were the first among their siblings (because they were so young) to have children. Thus, in many cases, these women were the first to break family traditions, such as where to spend Christmas. In response to a question regarding relationships with parents, one early-timing mother said:

> I was going to add what having a child did to our new family unit in relation to respective families that we grew up in. The three years we were married before we had children, we would go for Christmas to my parents and in-laws (Texas) every year. He had never left his home at Christmas, and we flew there at some point around the holidays. We were always with my parents (who lived nearby) for Christmas day. We continued these ties. We continued until last year when our daughter was one—then we decided it was too much—we had become our own unit—we can't be continuing as children in these families. It was real rough, not for my husband's family, because he has other sibs—but for my parents it was a very rough breaking point for them—to see their oldest now with a husband and a daughter saying, "We'll join you for certain holi-days for certain hours—it can't always be like it was when Judy was a little girl."

Other comments from early-timers supported this use of parenthood to facilitate the separation/individuation process from family of origin:

> We made that decision two years ago, and it was very painful on all sides because they didn't want to let go. They'd wait to open their presents until we got there. We had a two and one-half hour drive between the two sets of grandparents. It was extremely painful for my mother-in-law because her husband had died on Christmas Eve. Every year on Christmas Eve we got this tale of woe from her to come help her through this. Now it's coming up on nine years. We went there for seven years. We've now decided it's a holiday time for us to be at home and start new traditions. We stay put, and if they want to travel they come to us.

> We did that for the last time [traveled to parents' home]. We stayed home for the first time. We used to get together at my mother-in-law's on Christmas Eve. While it was nice, we had two babies and a long ride. We then rushed home to be with my parents one year. Last year we stayed at home and had an open house. . . . It worked out well.

> Two years ago we broke the tradition—we made the decision we wouldn't all get together for Christmas. We're now in our own family unit. It came at a good time, because everybody else started having children and I didn't have to struggle through that.

These comments illustrate how early-timers make use of the parenthood experience to facilitate their separation from the lifestyle and values of their own parents.

Late-timers more frequently discussed how their relationships with their mothers were enhanced by their own experience with parenthood. During one group discussion, they initiated the topic and wondered why I hadn't asked them more directly how their relationships with their mothers had changed since they had become parents themselves.[4] One 37-year-old mother with two preschool children said, "You start thinking a lot about your own mother when you become a mother." Many of the other older mothers agreed that they had definitely become more thoughtful regarding their relationships with their own mothers. One 35-year-old mother commented:

It [motherhood] has enhanced my relationship with my mother a great deal. I found that I really developed a great admiration for her. She had three children in three years and was always so relaxed in her attitude toward her children. She was always a bit dazed during these early years and always laid back regarding the whole thing. But then, she started off when she was twenty-five and that probably made some difference. But then, she's a lot more relaxed than I am in her attitude toward children. She doesn't get into all the psychology and the attitudes. She just figures that love and natural reactions to things get you through a lot of trouble and crises. We tend to look it up in a book or to worry about it in much greater dimensions.

Another mother, who is now 37, commented very poignantly:

Having a child has changed my relationship with my mother. Before having children, I was still trying to pull away and was afraid that she was going to succeed in making me like her. But now I need her and appreciate all the help that I used to hate. They live in another state.

Other late-timers added:

I will get more worked up about toys all over the floor but she [her mother] tends to be more relaxed. Disorder bothers me a lot more than it bothers her. My mother, who was twenty-five when she had kids, said she used to look at the ceiling a lot. She was less bothered by physical surroundings of things for a while.

Do you think that's because you were older when you had children?

Yes, yes.

You said something that caught my attention and that's the word *relaxed*—she was more relaxed. If I had to name one word I'm probably not—it's relaxed.

Thus, the experience of motherhood seems to have moved the early-timing mothers toward separation from their mothers, although their relationships are intense and conflicted. In contrast, the late-timing mothers, having already achieved and consolidated a sense of identity, can now sit back and reflect on their mothers as individuals in a more objective, empathic way. In a sense, parenthood has enhanced their relationships with their mothers because they appreciate them from an adult perspective.

Late-Timers Are More Comfortable with Dependency Needs

Statistical analysis indicated that late-timing mothers find it much easier (ANOVA, $p < .01$) to ask for help and support when they need it than early-timing mothers do. Late-timers appear to be more able and willing to reach out for much-needed external resources and social supports. For example, during the earliest phase of this study, when late-timing mothers were contacted by telephone, they were very excited about participating in small-group discussions, were pleased to offer their homes for meetings, and readily provided me with names of other late-timing mothers. Several late-timing mothers were extremely willing to drive a long distance to participate in a group discussion.

Moreover, these women seemed to derive more emotional gratification from the group discussions. They related to one another more easily, talked more readily, and more often exchanged names and addresses with other women in the group. My research assistant and I did not observe this same reaction from as many of the early-timing mothers. In general, it was more difficult to involve the younger women in the group discussion phase of the study. As the study results indicated, late-timers gave friendships a high priority in their lives.

In a longitudinal study of pregnancy, birth and parenthood, Grossman reported that the women who adjust most comfortably to pregnancy and the first year of an infant's life are those who can accept an increase in their own level of dependency. These are women who can ask for help when they need it without being frightened of this need. In addition, Grossman's study revealed that the woman's acceptance of her dependency needs can best be accomplished if she can ask for help from others and if her husband is able to hear her request and respond to it.[5]

This pattern was also reported by late-timing mothers in my study, suggesting that these women are more comfortable accepting their own dependency needs and their need for emotional support. Because late-timers are more sure of their own sense of autonomy, perhaps they can be more accepting of this dependent side of themselves. Early-timing mothers are more conflicted about asking for help because they are caught up in a struggle for separation from their own parents and have not yet developed a strong sense of self.

Marital Relationships and Family Patterns

The late-timing mothers in this study had been married for an average of 7.5 years, although there was a wide range from 2 to 14.5 years. The early-timing mothers had been married an average of 5.5 years, with a range from 1 year to 9 years. Most of the early-timers were married at age 21 or 22 and had their first children within two years of their marriage. The late-timing mothers had married at about age 27 and had waited, on the average, five years to have their first child. These averages can be misleading, however, because of the wide range in the number of years married.

Although the late-timing mothers had been married approximately two years longer than the early-timing mothers, the important point seems to be that the women who waited to have children also waited to get married. In fact, several late-timers commented that they could not have pictured themselves becoming involved in a long-term relationship during their twenties. The late-timers were women who had spent their twenties developing a work interest or furthering their education.

The timing of parenthood as it relates to marriage is not the main focus of this book.[6] However, some interesting and important data emerged during the small-group discussions that confirm and broaden the conclusions provided by other researchers on this topic. Both early- and late-timing mothers reported that parenthood represents a significant adjustment in the lifestyle of the marital couple. On a Likert-type scale—with choices of "extreme," "moderate," "not very much," and "no change'—50 percent of the early-timing mothers rated this adjustment "moderate," and more than half of the late-timing mothers (65.8 percent) rated it "moderate." It is noteworthy that more than 25 percent of both groups believed that parenthood creates an "extreme" change in the couple's lifestyle. In both groups of mothers, there was a perception that adjustment to parenthood is more difficult for the couple than it is for the mother herself. Most women reported that, following parenthood, household responsibilities are increased for a couple and that they spend considerably less time alone together.

The following statements by both early- and late-timing mothers describe the general adjustments that the couple has made to parenthood.

> We spend considerably less time alone together. Our household responsibilities increased—more wash, additional meal planning.

> We began to organize more "family" kinds of activities.

> We focus on child and parenting much more than on our relationship.

However, upon more careful examination of the data, it is clear that, for a typical late-timing mother, parenthood provides more of an opportunity for an expanded relationship with her husband. One 33-year-old mother of an 8-month-old daughter said:

> I think one of the advantages for Carl and me was having talked about our feelings—including our scary ones—about what it would mean to have a child—what having a child would mean to our relationship. What I realize is that if we had really pushed it (I was ready before Carl was) before both of us were equally ready—it would have been a breach of trust and commitment. I see that the longer we've been together, the more we've grown to trust one another—levels of commitment. That's been one of the wonderful things about having Matthew—is this new way of being deeper and closer together and connected.

This response seems in direct contrast to that of a 24-year-old mother, whose experience is similar to that of many early-timing parents who do not seem to be so open in their expression of feelings with one another:

> When I was doing my questionnaire [for this study], I kind of left it out on purpose, because I don't talk about those things that much with my husband. There are things I'd like to talk to him about, but I guess I don't have the nerve. He read part of it and he asked me questions about it and he didn't like

some of my answers. I pointed out the good answers, but I was wondering how many of the women that came shared it [the questionnaire] with their husbands. I was glad to have an opportunity on paper for him to see some of my feelings—what was going on up here [she pointed to her head]. You know, you just don't come out and say "Oh, Tom, I really feel—or I think this—or we're really changing so much."

When the data from the small-group discussions were examined in more depth, further interesting differences in family and marital patterns emerged. Whereas early-timing mothers tend to "take care of their husband's needs" as well as those of their children, late-timing mothers tend to be involved in a more egalitarian relationship with their husbands, in which the men participate in child care and household tasks. One woman, who was 33 years old at the birth of her first child, indicated how important it is to her to have a supportive, egalitarian marital relationship—one in which both husband and wife share in child rearing and in the household tasks:

If we had been married ten years before, it would have been a very different time in terms of relationships and women. My sister married exactly ten years before I did, and she was married at a time when you jumped up to get your husband a cup of coffee or whatever he wanted, and she still does that. Ten years later, things had changed enough and I had thought about it enough when we got married so that I knew that was not what I wanted when I got married. I really think that part of being a parent is the support system and part of the system is your spouse. I just feel that if my husband didn't do housework and didn't do cooking and didn't take care of the kids a lot—if he didn't share all that with me—I would be a very different kind of parent. That's been a very crucial part of it, and I'm glad that I didn't get married at twenty.

A 37-year-old mother of two children remarked that her marital relationship has been established on a more equitable basis because both partners had a "life of their own" before the arrival of children.

Having been married and working for a while before kids, my husband was used to the way I lived my life previous to children. It doesn't disturb him to fall back to that kind of life. If we had been married right after college, he may have had different expectations of a wife—that I was going to be there all the time with a wonderful dinner at 6.00 P.M. He has never said you have to go to work or not. It's easier to go back to the life I had before. The mothers I know who had children earlier seem to have demanding husbands. Their husbands play baseball four times per week while the wife is home with the kids.

Our husbands did change because they saw us develop as people and stand on our own two feet. Our husbands lived on their own for a while before marriage and they know that we know that.

The women who had delayed childbearing indicated that their husbands enjoyed caring for their children while their wives worked or went out for an evening.

This more egalitarian pattern in a late-timing family can be contrasted with the more paternalistic style of the early-timing families, in which the mothers often reported that they were on "child duty" morning, noon, and night. According to many of these mothers, when their husbands came home from work, they would eat dinner and then go out with friends or play ball. Many early-timing mothers reported that their husbands resisted taking care of the children, making it difficult for these women to have a much-needed break. In the following excerpt from a group discussion, several young mothers report how difficult this type of relationship can be for them in their role as parents:

If you go out and they [husbands] watch the kids, that's "babysitting," but what we do all day is not babysitting.

And that's all they do is watch the kids—they don't do the dishes or pick up the toys.

I was pregnant and had gone to the doctor's. I came home to find the other kids sound asleep on the floor in their clothes. I said to him, "You couldn't have put them in their pajamas?"

What happens in our house is—I ask my husband to do something and he refuses—there are times when he says no and I say, "How can you say that, you're their father?" I shouldn't have to request it—it is just as much his duty as it is mine. This shouldn't be—I shouldn't have to ask him to do something and he shouldn't have the option of saying no.

If my husband knew he had to care for kids regularly, we couldn't live together.

My husband doesn't have the patience as I do. He is away from them all day and they do something to upset him and he goes crazy. I can take it [the children's antics]. Sometimes it's better if he's not around, because it gets everything all shaken up.

Other young mothers agreed that the weekends are "tough." On weekends in some early-timing families, mothers and children spend many hours together while the fathers are working or sharing leisure time with their friends. One of the raters who analyzed the group discussion data remarked that, for early-timing mothers, the children are "more important than the spouse in this period of child rearing. There is very little cooperation between spouses; it is almost as if the marital relationship is put on hold."

Thus, it appears that in early-timing families, the mother–child unit is much stronger, and the father occupies a more isolated role. Motherhood appears to be the primary source of identity for early-timing mothers. These women see themselves functioning first as mothers and then as partners in a marriage.

Generational boundaries are a way of conceptualizing relationships or subsystems within a family so that we can understand what is happening. For example, within a family, we speak of a "boundary" between parents and children when we are considering who participates in particular transactions. A boundary between parents and children is weak in a family where children are too often drawn into adult interactions. In another family, the boundary between mother and children may be weak when the mother and children form a unit in which the father is kept out of the interactions and may be in an isolated role.[7] Analysis of the data from my study suggests that in many early-timing families, the generational boundaries between parents and children were breached. The early-timing mother and her children fulfill each other's needs, but the father occupies a more isolated role within the family.

In contrast, within late-timing families, mother, child, and father function as one unit, and parents put forth a reciprocal effort to meet each other's needs and to achieve a balance between care giving and care getting.[8] On weekends, mother, father, and child often spend time together in an activity. Within these families, the generational boundaries between mother and child are preserved, because late-timing mothers are better able to differentiate between meeting their own needs and meeting those of their children. Furthermore, late-timers reported that their husbands share in child care. Their marital relationships appear to be more equalized in terms of care giving and care getting. As mentioned in the preceding chapter, late-timers are also skilled at meeting their own needs and do not depend on their children as much as younger mothers do.

However, although the findings indicate that the egalitarian pattern in late-timing families encourages the father to become more involved in child care and homemaking, responses from late-timing mothers disclose that in many cases, the mother still assumes the psychological burden of parenting. As one late-timer commented:

> One thing we haven't talked about is the pent-up anger that I have felt toward my husband. I never got mad at my infant—it's not her fault that she needed me morning, noon, and night. My husband goes to work and has a nice lunch. I'm home and haven't seen an adult or read a paper. When my husband comes home, he sits and reads the paper. I can't sit down. I have a good, supportive husband who cooks dinner and was very excited about having a child. He thinks he's adorable and plays with him.

There is some similarity between that statement and one from a 25-year-old mother who expressed her frustration in having total responsibility for the children:

> I think one of the most difficult things I've found—I get a lot of help from my husband as far as taking care of the kids—but yet somehow I am still the primary caretaker. I'm totally in charge and it's when things really get to a peak that my husband will step in and help out and yell. I could have done that myself, and I didn't need him to yell after I've spent ten hours with the kids. You feel that he should at least be compassionate since he's only been with them for a few hours. I'm always in charge of getting a baby sitter and deciding where we go.

Summary

It is clear that there are many differences between early-timing and late-timing mothers with regard to the support systems they seek out to help them cope with the difficult task of motherhood. Friendships with other women seem more important to late-timing mothers, whereas early-timers are more dependent on their own mothers and sisters for emotional and physical caretaking. In general, late-timers seem to be more comfortable expressing their dependency needs and can ask for help when they need it. Furthermore, for late-timers, parenthood appears to facilitate a deepening of the marital relationship and friendships. For some early-timers, parenthood facilitates an emotional separation and individuation from their families of origin. Early-timers and late-timers agree, however, on the importance of obtaining physical and emotional support from outside the nuclear family during the years they are parenting preschool children.

7

The Ultimate Juggling Act: Work and Motherhood

A LTHOUGH none of the routine questions asked during the group discussions related to work outside the home, the late-timing mothers
were eager to discuss this issue. During my discussions with early-
timing mothers, the work issue rarely emerged as a topic of interest. Consequently, most of this chapter is devoted to comments by late-timers as they
explore the work issue. For example, one 32-year-old mother said:

> I'm Diane and I have a child who is six months old. . . . I resigned my job after
> taking a leave. . . . I decided I wouldn't be going back for a while because my
> work took me to Washington, which is too far to commute from Philadelphia.
> I'm in a situation of wondering when to go back—trying to find a new job in
> the new year—whether to go back part time—what type of day care. I've
> enjoyed these six months very much. I feel in conflict between wanting to stay
> home and wanting to get back into the career—I look forward to a discussion
> tonight.

Statistics on Working Outside the Home

At the time they were interviewed, almost twice as many late-timing
mothers were working outside the home (almost half) as early-timing
mothers (about one-quarter) (see table 1). The small percentage of early-
timing mothers who work outside the home may indicate that they have
made different choices with respect to work following the birth of their
children.

However, it is very interesting and significant that equal percentages of both groups (59 percent) have worked outside the home at *some* point since having children. At the time they were interviewed, more late-timing mothers reported that they were working outside the home. Thus, it is probable that many of the early-timing mothers who returned to work after childbirth have decided to return to homemaking. According to the data generated in this study, the two groups of women had similar female role models with regard to combining work and family. Equal percentages of the mothers of the women in both the early-timing and the late-timing groups worked (49 percent) and did not work (51 percent) during the participants' childhoods.

Balancing Motherhood and Work

Other factors must account for the different patterns of combining work and motherhood among early- and late-timing mothers. Early-timing mothers may remain at home while their children are pre-schoolers because of their limited education and training. Some of them put their careers "on hold" so that their husbands could advance in *their* careers. A young mother of two, who was 20 when her first child was born, commented:

> When my son was two, we started to plan a career change for my husband to go to medical school, so we started to prepare two years ago. I had two years of college to go, so the idea was for me to return and get my degree so I could support the family while he was in med school. We put the kids in day care and I took courses. Two weeks into it, my youngest one (the two-year-old) quit talking, sleeping, and eating and stopped being potty trained. It was just horrible, and we had to make a decision. I decided to pull him out of day care and got him a babysitter so as to not throw that money away. But I decided to only go to school that one term and go back to being a full-time Mommy to him because he couldn't handle it. So here it is two years later and I don't have my degree and can't support us. I don't know what I'll do, but I don't regret it because those two years I could never have back—he's now a happy, well-adjusted kindergartner.

It is significant that this young mother reported that she returned to being a "full-time Mommy" because her son "couldn't handle it." I suspect that this mother also had difficulty keeping herself together as a separate person while caring for a small child who was making many emotional demands. As noted earlier, it is especially difficult for early-timing mothers to maintain a sense of separateness from their preschool children.

Late-timing mothers are likely to be better educated and better trained for a career or job. This makes it easier for them to consider staying in, or returning to, the job market once they have children. These women also tend to have fewer children than early-timing mothers, so it may be easier for them to cope with the tensions of work and motherhood.

These findings suggest that women who delay childbirth past the age of 30 may be more comfortable integrating work and motherhood. This conclusion supports research on female adult development that suggests that, developmentally, it is much easier for women to combine work/career and motherhood in their thirties than in their twenties.[1] The following comments from two young mothers (aged 21 and 22, respectively, when their first children were born) explain why it may be more difficult for younger women to balance the roles of worker and mother:

> I enjoyed working part-time, but my husband didn't like it so I had to give it up. I enjoyed being a working mother. It didn't work with a family life—it was too hard for my husband to come home from work and make dinner.

> If I have a sick kid, how would I work? My husband would never stay home with a sick kid [laughter and head nodding from other mothers in the group]. My husband is just not for taking care of children. He loves them, but they're my responsibility—that makes a difference.

From these comments, we can surmise that support from one's spouse is critical in juggling motherhood and career. The age of fathers may also be important in how mothers work out the struggle of parenthood and selfhood. Older fathers (those in their middle to upper thirties) are usually more stabilized in a career and have more time, energy, and desire to help with housework and child care. As noted in chapter 6, the husbands of late-timing mothers share in household work and child care much more frequently than the spouses of the early-timers do.

One young woman, who was 23 when her first child was born, described her dilemma as a full-time graduate student and a mother:

> One thing I'd like to add about having a child at this time is the extra juggling and balancing in our life. I started my master's degree the year I got pregnant and decided I didn't want to keep going as full-time as I had been before. I wanted to have that special close time with her, so I took off that time and have just started back completing my degree this year—she is a two-year-old

now. What am I going to do after finishing the degree—put her in day care? Will I continue to postpone having another child or do I want to have another child? Where does the career come in then? All of that balancing and timing is a great challenge right now. How do I balance a career with kids? Especially for a woman like me who wants to have a career focus and rear small children.

It is interesting that this woman contacted me after the study to let me know what had happened to her with regard to this dilemma. After her graduation, she and her husband decided to have another child. Six months after the birth of her second child, she found a part-time job near her home. However, after six months on the job, she decided to leave her work, because the demands of two young children and even a part-time job were too difficult for her to manage without feeling exhausted and guilt-ridden.

In contrast to the comments from the early-timing mothers, who had trouble considering both work and motherhood, a late-timing mother who is a social worker reported:

I'm Susan and we have two children—two girls—Jane is almost five and Carrie is a little over two. I was working full time before Jane was born and then went to two and one-half days. When Carrie was born, I went to one day per week. I've been lucky enough to have a flexible enough babysitter and a flexible enough job so that the day switches sometimes and the amount of work is never overwhelming. I'm in social services, and I guess I sort of made a commitment to go back full-time when their budget improves.

Many late-timing mothers appreciated the advantages of having flexible full-time or part-time positions, which they were able to negotiate because their six or seven years of work experience before the birth of their first children had placed them in a strong bargaining position with their employers. Younger mothers who time the birth of their first children right after attaining a high school or college degree do not have this same advantage and do not feel the same sense of power or control over their lives with regard to the job market. Many early-timing mothers voiced a desire to enter or return to the job market but felt unskilled and powerless in that arena. This concern was not voiced by late-timing mothers.

Late-timing mothers seemed to have more clearly differentiated the roles of worker and mother, which helped them to cope with the stresses of each role. Several mothers said that they were able to separate their identities as worker and mother to handle the delicate balance involved in mothering. As one 38-year-old mother with one child said:

What's really strange is that I can sort of separate myself into the mother-at-home, the teacher-at-school. I've had a chance to do some substitute teaching in the fall, and it was really good. I would leave her with a babysitter and I always had faith that it was going to be OK. She's with good people, and then I would go about my job and I'd think about her at break time and wonder what Judy is doing. Other than that I didn't think about her, because I was totally wrapped up in teaching and I was glad to be teaching—it was really something other than changing a diaper. As soon as that bell rang, I was out that door and couldn't wait to get back to her—at the slightest traffic jam I was furious. When I was teaching it was really great. I didn't think about her at all—I could really separate the two identities.

For late-timing mothers, a well-defined sense of identity and an ability to integrate various components of their lives are clearly related to their capacity to meet their children's needs while, at the same time, holding on to their sense of self.

Late-Timing Mothers Ask: Do I Want to Work at All?

If it is, indeed, easier for a woman to combine work and motherhood in her thirties than in her twenties, why were less than half of the late-timers in this study (46 percent) working? And even more perplexing, why are only a small percentage of those late-timers who are employed (24 percent) working full-time? Although the women who participated in my study may not be representative of the population at large, it is interesting and significant that my findings confirm what others have found and are continuing to find as they research the lives of women who are delaying childbearing and coping with the dilemma of work and motherhood.

In Deane Foltz's study, women who had delayed their careers to have children first claimed that their careers were more important at the time they were interviewed. In contrast, the women who indicated that motherhood was more important now were those who had delayed motherhood to work on a career in their twenties: "In anticipation of and in the actual experience of being a mother, [they] felt more strongly about it than ever before." In the Foltz study, more than 80 percent of the "delayers" reported the main change in a woman's life after having her first child as "Being a mother became a satisfying and fulfilling part of my life."[2]

Both the statistical analysis and the qualitative data from my study support these findings. As noted in chapter 5, late-timing mothers more frequently ranked their children as the number one source of satisfaction in their lives.

This sense of satisfaction with motherhood is apparent in the following self-introductions of two late-timers in one of the small-group discussions. The first comment was from a woman who had only been a mother for 11 months:

> I'm Nancy and I have an almost eleven-month-old daughter and I'm not working and I have no plans to work. I don't have to work economically. I did have plans before I gave birth to go back to work—I thought part-time. I had worked for ten years and couldn't see myself staying home. It was a surprise to find myself fulfilled and satisfied—sometimes—a lot of times a little bored and the craving for some free time to myself. Basically I'm happy with what I'm doing and feel that it's the right thing for me. The biggest problem in my life is trying to find other things, aside from working, which will add a little more to my life. I'm looking into different volunteer things and right now we're planning on moving to the suburbs. . . . Right now I'm pretty happy.

The following remark was from a mother who had been away from her career for 5 years but was still very satisfied with motherhood:

> I'm Karen and I have Jamie who's five years old and Brian who is eighteen months. I'm a social worker and I kind of left it open as to whether I'd go back or not. I haven't worked in five years, and I don't feel any great urge to get a job. I've been doing volunteer work—teaching parenting skills—and I've done some volunteer work in my son's school where there is a need for parents to come in. I guess I see this as my time to find out who I am apart from my job. I worked as a social worker for ten years and that was a big piece of my life and I'm kind of interested to see what happens when it's taken away. I feel happy with it. I guess having a child start school makes you realize how very quickly those first five years go. It seems like just yesterday that he was an infant.

One late-timer spoke of her satisfaction with motherhood:

> I think that in a positive way I've felt like you [to another mother]—that it [motherhood] is an exciting and challenging job—it's also that it has helped me to get through some of the frustrating stuff. I remind myself that this is probably the most challenging job I'll ever have in my life. I'll use myself physically, emotionally, intellectually more being a mother to Sam than in any paid job I've ever had.

Daniels and Weingarten also found that women who postponed parenthood had every expectation that motherhood would interfere with their work, but they were surprised by the shift in their feelings toward their work once the baby was born. These women had not counted on "being enthralled" by their children and found that "it was their jobs that interfered with their mothering and not the other way around."[3]

After interviewing several couples who had delayed parenthood well into their thirties, Wolfe reported that what was most striking was that these parents had been "shaken to their roots by love and that, despite all their preparation for parenthood, the love has come as something of a shock." A prominent woman in publishing reported: "It's all such a big surprise. I mean, the emotional attachment you feel toward a child."[4] In a *New York Times Magazine* article, Anita Schreve reported that many mothers who have delayed childbirth into their thirties are not returning to their careers. If they do return, it is on a part-time basis, which interfaces with the care of their children. As one professional woman who was interviewed declared:

> You have to sacrifice. If you want to have dinner with your kids at six, you can't be on a high-powered track. . . . To sacrifice a few years out of your career at age thirty is nothing in the long run. You sacrifice more if you don't. I'm often very nostalgic about the lost moments of Nathaniel's childhood.[5]

In Shreve's words, "Many working mothers reject the concept of Superwoman. They fear that their juggling act is too costly to their career, their children and their marriages."[6]

Similarly, a 37-year-old mother in my study commented:

> I think that's one of the problems that the feminist movement got us into—they expected us all to become supermoms. It's only just now that we're pulling out of that and allowing ourselves to relax and say "who cares?"—take off some years and enjoy being a mother. Get back into it any which way you can or care to—don't feel pressured into having to do this dual thing [motherhood and career].

In the following excerpt from a group discussion with ten late-timing mothers, there is further evidence of a rebellion against the superwoman model as well as anger at being labeled "just a mother":

> One of the things I really have trouble with, having been a professional person in a position of some authority and a statusy thing—to hear people say things like "Oh, you're just a mother." To me it's very important to be a mother. But

then it's Madison Avenue business—first they sell you this bill of goods on this fabulous job.

Sometimes you feel like you're just a mother—when you're with certain people.

But, aha, you shouldn't.

You shouldn't—but it's hard when you've worked all those years to feel really good about it—to project that.

It's shifting in this country. For the last four years women have been getting back into the job market in droves—fifty percent of women who are mothers are working—as reported in the newspapers. And they went through the whole supermom situation—women can do it all at work and at home. That was about two years ago, and then last year I noticed it started shifting. It began to be said that they can't do it all—it's impossible. Beverly Sills gave a graduation speech and said "No, you can't have it all—you have to choose, because you're the one who suffers in the end—you're tired all the time." I was interested in how this is beginning to shift so that you are allowed to be a mother at home without feeling guilty. But I've found it very hard to say "Well, I'm a Spanish teacher—I feel very proud of this"—to somebody saying to you "What do you do?" I say "Well, I'm at home." They say "Well, what do you really do—besides that?"

Several late-timers remarked that they were content to stay at home with their children because they had worked for a number of years before motherhood and had "gotten that out of their system."

I think because I was thirty when I had a family— it was an easier decision for me to stop working because I had an opportunity to teach for seven years. I had spent all those years with other children and I was ready to spend time with my own children. I could take a break and that helped me to make a decision.

A lot of women who have worked for several years have felt that they worked long enough—they have done what they've obviously wanted to do in the working world and now they're ready to stay home. Whereas women who had children at an earlier age never really felt they had a chance to get out there and work—to be—and to do the things that they really wanted to do—or maybe never had the money—the financial aspect of it too—with your husband and you both working.

As other researchers and I have found, late-timers discover that motherhood propels them to "reprioritize" their career aspirations. The late-timing mothers in my study frequently commented that, although their work or career is still important to them, their relationship with their children has a higher priority for them now. The following responses of three late-timers to a question about the most significant way in which parenthood has changed their lives illustrate the feelings of many of the late-timers:

A 32-year-old woman with a 2-year-old child who is now a full-time homemaker: It [parenthood] has challenged me to look at myself in a new way. I've always defined myself largely in relation to my profession without realizing it. Now I'm looking more at myself as a wife and mother.

A 33-year-old woman with a 10-month-old baby who is now a full-time homemaker: I was pleasantly surprised to find motherhood so satisfying. I do not feel the need to find stimulation by working (luckily, we do not need the money). I feel much more protective of my child than I thought I would and do not want to leave her on a regular basis with someone else.

A 35-year-old mother with two preschoolers who is working part-time as a planner: It changes what I think is most important to me — kids first, then husband and my work.

According to these women, their work lives must now be reorganized around this very important person in their lives. Two late-timing mothers make this very clear in the following comments regarding the positive effects motherhood has had on their work lives:

I'm wondering if it isn't work that comes easier because it's not as important. It's not the only thing you're doing.

Everything isn't invested in it. It's important, but sometimes I get mad at my kids for invading work, but it's more like I get mad at work. It's not your whole identity.

A newspaper article confirmed this trend among women who have been career-oriented in their twenties, reporting that a number of frustrated female professionals have decided to take a break from their careers and stay at home. Marion Frank, who specializes in the problems of professional women, is quoted: "There's a certain amount of disenchantment with the feminist movement. Women are redefining what success is for them."[7]

Many women who chose careers over relationships in their twenties and early thirties are feeling unfulfilled. Some of these women are similar to the late-timing mothers I interviewed who stated that motherhood brought out the more nurturing, relationship-oriented personality traits they had so long neglected.

Some Late-Timing Mothers are Frustrated Without a "Work Identity"

Although a vocal group of late-timers said that they enjoy staying home with their children another group seemed frustrated because they lack what they called a "work-identity." Several late-timing mothers explored the importance of a "work identity" for them. One 36-year-old mother who has three daughters discussed the importance of her work as a role model for them and also as a valuable experience for her:

> I feel real good about having something concrete. Since I have three daughters, I can be a role model—not that any of them have to do what I'm doing but just that they can watch me doing something and achieving and participating and having an identity. . . . Role models have been important to me in my own search for my identity, but I feel so good when I think about doing that and I can't imagine doing it [working] if I'd been in my twenties when I had my children. I would have been restless and frustrated and a lot of things that I don't feel. For me it's been a valuable experience.

Two other late-timers discussed how difficult it has been for them to function in their new role as a mother without being employed outside the home.

> I think there is a danger in staying away from work too long because I stopped work—I'm a counselor—when I got pregnant—my doctor felt at my age and wanting a pregnancy so much it was dumb to risk being exposed to the school-children—I never had rubella. I stopped work then and figured it didn't really matter because I had my whole dissertation to write. . . . I'm two years down the road and I'm just picking it up again. I haven't worked for three years, and I already see something insidious happening to me—even though I worked for fourteen years. I have a work identity as a teacher, and as a counselor. I stopped working for three years and I'm already beginning to feel that I'm just a mother and that I have no skills—I have no competence. . . . I can't believe that could happen to me when I've been so busy doing such real things in the real world out there. There is a big part of me that is nervous about getting a job—

those things that I saw mothers struggling with years ago who had never had a work identity suddenly attacked me after years of working. I would not have believed that that would have happened to me and it has. I feel that it is crucial that I get back to work sometime soon.

I've had the same feelings, and I haven't worked in five years. I really think that it says something about us as women — that our identities are so fragile. Someone said recently that we've been "en masse" in the work force and it's kind of like you're not a respectable person. Here the men are being applauded for being house-husbands — I know a few men who have made decisions to stay home and everybody says "Isn't that wonderful." Here I am shaking in my boots and afraid someone is thinking I'm not a total person. That's something that I've really tried to work on myself — that I'm very much the same person whether or not I'm at work. [At this point, many other group members chimed in with "It's hard."]

The following comment is from the same woman who had stated earlier that she was doing a full-time job in part-time hours. This statement illustrates the feelings of many other late-timers who reported that motherhood has given them an opportunity to explore another aspect of their identity:

For me that's the negative of having a work identity. I'm trying to wrestle with that right now. I turned down a full-time job. I'd been working for a long time and I want a part-time job. . . . It was a real struggle. . . . I'm glad from the point of view of having a little peace — being able to find something else that isn't so straining. But at the same time my identity is so tied up in a job. I'm a little bit afraid of who I am if I don't have this job. Do I have any value if I don't have a job that I can say that I can do? There is a danger of saying a work identity is good, because you've got to keep it in perspective. Now the other identity really needs some work.

Concerns of Women Who Are Juggling Work and Motherhood

The late-timing mothers who were working at the time they participated in the study discussed some of the difficulties they were having in balancing their love of both career and family. Women who have waited until their thirties to have a child and who are well established in their careers are often more deeply invested in both career and motherhood than younger women. This double bind becomes especially intense and probably contributes to the stress for these women in adjusting to parenthood.[8] A 35-year-old mother, who works for a radio station and has an 11-month-old daughter, returned to work when her daughter was 4-months old. She discussed her conflict with work and motherhood:

> That's the whole reason that I went back to work—I have a job that's a pretty unique job—I like it a great deal. If I didn't and when I don't like it, I say I'm going to quit tomorrow. I couldn't duplicate it—there's only one position like it in town and I've got it. When I leave that job I'll just do something else. . . . The decision [returning to work] was hard for me, and I tried to negotiate a part-time position. I worked overtime before I left and finally got an assistant—so me working overtime didn't fly. You're not overworked now and you don't think you'll be overworked when you come back. I went back on a trial basis and I'm still there—but as far as I'm concerned, every month it's a trial, and it's a month-to-month thing. My baby keeps getting cuter. If I didn't like it a lot, I wouldn't be there. I would feel like my priorities were all wrong being there. My attitude is different once I get there. . . . I really knock myself out at work more than I did before I left, because before I left I was kind of preoccupied with the baby. Now I figure if I'm going to be here, I better be able to justify it to myself—I'm a lot more committed. But when I leave [work], I get this new surge of energy—because I'm really excited about getting home.

Many late-timers wanted to discuss balancing their desire for a work identity and their desire to spend quality time with their children. During one group session, a 34-year-old mother with a young infant led off the discussion:

> I'm Connie, and Sam is four months old and still not sleeping through the night [Connie and the other mothers laughed at this point]—he's notorious in our play group. I was interested in participating in this study because I'm concerned about combining my work with being a mother. I'm a psychotherapist—I'm trying to get a private practice going and the hassles with that and the adjustment to being a new mother. I found it real difficult and was looking forward to the opportunity of meeting other women who are struggling with the same thing. It's hard.

Another mother introduced herself as follows:

> My name is Carol, and I have a nine-month-old daughter named Judith. I'm lucky because she's been sleeping through the night since six weeks. It's been helpful, because since then I've been working for a corporation—I'm a financial analyst. I've been doing my full-time job in part-time hours but the job will end at the end of the year. I turned down a full-time position because a part-time

position was hassle enough. I would like to go back and find a true part-time position—one where I don't have to come home and worry about the things that are still going on at work and to be able to focus on my daughter or things around the house. It sounds like everyone has to deal with the work issue.

The last woman to introduce herself really has her hands full with three young children (including a newborn infant). She is struggling with her commitment to the ministry and motherhood:

I'm Sandra, and I have three children—ages five, two, and three weeks. I've worked—I'm a minister and I've worked full-time—after each child, taking up to a year off—that's the longest time in between. This last child was not planned and came as something of a jolt. Currently, I'm on maternity leave and anticipating being back at work—part-time after the first of the year. I have a period of time to see how things are going—and gradually working full-time again. That's very flexible, and I'm fortunate because I'm feeling a lot of anxiety about trying to work full-time with three children. Even though it worked fairly well before, because I have flexible hours—it's not a 9:00 to 5:00 situation. Currently, I'm one of several ministers on the staff of a large church, which helps with the work load. Right now I'm feeling anxiety about working full-time and a lot of ambivalence about that in spite of how important it's been to me before—and also something that you need, which is less true than in the past.

Summary

For both early- and late-timing mothers, combining the roles of mother and worker outside the home brings struggles, concerns, and anxieties. Yet it appears that women who have delayed having children until their thirties are more frequently able to blend part-time work with caring for preschool children. This seems true partly because they have prepared themselves during their early adulthood by establishing skills that they can market to an employer on a part-time basis. But it may just be easier for them to "do it all" because of the developmental growth that occurs during the middle and late twenties. This growth prepares a woman to better handle the struggles of work and motherhood because she has a more well developed sense of who she is. Late-timers also benefit from spouses who are generally more supportive and who share in the household chores. Furthermore, late-timers have moved closer to balancing the self–other tensions that are part of adult development.

However, many of these late-timers have chosen to put their careers on hold for a while, because motherhood has become infectious for them. They are caught up in the thrill of watching their young children grow and develop into people. Other late-timers are frustrated because they do not have a work identity to help them balance their sense of self as they struggle with the demands that young children make on their lives.

8

The Mothers Speak Out: The Advantages and Disadvantages of Timing

R EGARDLESS of the timing of her first baby, parenthood provides the mother an opportunity to enhance her growth and development as a person. Along these lines, it is interesting that there were no significant differences between early- and late-timing mothers regarding their degree of satisfaction with the choice they made as to the timing of the birth of their first children. Both groups were eager to discuss the advantages and disadvantages of the timing of their first children.[1]

Some of the disadvantages late-timers presented included their concerns about their own aging and the possibility that they might not live to watch their children graduate from college or get married or to be involved with their grandchildren. As a 36-year-old woman remarked:

Everything is more precious. Will I still be around when my child goes through a certain life cycle event—how long am I going to be here?

Many late-timers reported that this concern with age affects their planning and sense of time. They are more conscious of wanting to make every day count for themselves and their children. A 37-year-old mother commented:

As you get older, you have an increasing awareness of the value of time—so much to learn. You feel you must transfer as much knowledge to your child as quickly as possible—I spend a lot of time boring my child.

With this increased awareness of time may come an increased appreciation for their children but also an increased pressure to squeeze as much as possible into a perceived shorter space of time.

Other age-related concerns voiced by late-timers were that being an older parent means that "you have less physical energy to keep up with the child's energy level" and that "getting up in the middle of the night is harder the older you grow." Two late-timers commented along this line:

My energy level is a disadvantage. There is no way I can keep up with my child's energy level. I had to put him some place where he could burn it off. I wasn't going to run around the block with him—nursery school did that for him. He came home and could do quiet things with me.

There is a disadvantage of being older—physically, I'm not as young as I used to be. When I was younger, I did play with little kids—running and jumping. Getting up in the middle of the night when you're over thirty-five is not easy. My second child didn't sleep through the night for eighteen months—ear infections, etc. As you get older, it gets harder to stay up and have energy during the day. When I was young, I used to go all night and day.

On the other side of the coin, late-timers perceived a number of advantages in delayed parenthood. Most of these advantages clustered around the fact that these women had a better sense of themselves when they became parents. Also, because they had spent their twenties exploring alternative roles for themselves, they didn't feel as though they'd missed out on an important part of life, and they experience more contentment with their role as mothers. The following excerpt from a discussion with late-timing mothers reveals this attitude:

I have always loved children and have been good around children, but I can't imagine that I would have been as good a mother in my twenties as I am now. I was really still a kid. One of the big, big advantages of having children when you're older is your understanding of children and your patience. And your understanding of yourself [agreement from other mothers].

And you don't feel like you're missing things—if you don't get to the party or you miss the movies.

If we had had children in our twenties, I wouldn't have known better—I wouldn't have known the freedom of my own time—the happiness of my work. People who are younger think they've missed something and are ready to get out and do something now.

One advantage is that you probably develop some sort of your own identity—whether we're working or not we've figured that out. I think most younger parents have not gone through that. The father may have developed some of that [identity], but they've still got their collegiate identity. I had an identity . . . before I got married that had nothing to do with my kids or my husband, but is all me—I think that's really important, and younger parents don't have that.

I would agree. My older sister chose to have her children right after she got married in her early twenties—her kids are twelve and fourteen. She never had a career and she's struggling with that now—I have already worked that out for myself. I'm having a hassle trying to fit it all together, but I think I have it easier. She's really having a tough time now, and I feel bad for her. She's over-invested in her kids. If the only thing you're doing is taking care of kids—if that's your sole identity—it's like the bride who burned the peas—you have nothing to make you feel good about yourself—if you fail with your kids.

The other big advantage that late-timers reported was having more money available so that they can meet more of their own needs and those of their children:

Money is a positive factor in that we can afford to have a maid service and babysitters. We do overindulge.

I'm surprised that no one has brought up money. Usually when you have children later you are more stable and in a better financial position. . . . Usually that is a big advantage of having children late—your stability.

Several other late-timers agreed that having a stable financial situation allowed them more choices for themselves:

With the way the economy is now—waiting and getting your house and saving money—enables you to make a choice as to whether or not you want to go back to work or not. Maybe some of the younger girls have to go back. Waiting gives you more choices.

Late-timers also agreed that delaying parenthood gave them a better perspective on time, which helped them cope with the frustrations that come with motherhood:

When you get to be thirty, you know that nothing lasts forever. You can look at childhood and say that this child is taking up all my time right now, but it's only going to be a couple of years—they're going to be in school and things are going to open up again. Having the advantage of age gives you maturity.

I find it easier to be completely involved with children, having traveled, worked . . . you know, having done some of the things I wanted to do.

Any things that we haven't done that I'd like to do I don't feel that we have to do right now. I was ready at that point to stay home. Eventually those opportunities may come—I don't feel frustrated. I feel I would have felt that way [frustrated] having a child at twenty-one or twenty-two.

Much of the frustration expressed by early-timing mothers seemed to emanate from their impatience with certain stages of their children's development—particularly the "terrible twos." These women did not have the same perspective as the late-timers—that this stage would pass.

Late-timers have fewer fantasies about the world of work outside the home, having spent their twenties employed in jobs. As one late-timing mother reported:

Well, you know the limitations of having done it [working]. What's an eighty-hour week? Having just been out in the world and having done things, you can say, "Well, if you had stayed home at twenty-one—my career—well, you know where that's at—writing proposals in the dead of the night—staying up with the baby in the dead of the night is just as easy."

A 37-year-old mother with two preschoolers summed it up:

I think you're thrown at other ages. It's not just at thirty but at twenty-three or twenty-one—motherhood is a shock to your system. At thirty-five, you're more mature and able to handle it—at least I felt that I was. I was ready to nest. I felt that I had worked and put my career on hold. I thought we were in a better financial position to have a child—in being able to get out and hire baby-sitters—you do have the money. You're able to get out on Saturday nights. When you're twenty-one or twenty-two, you don't have the money—you're stuck in the house—your outlook is pretty bleak, and you may become depressed.

Early-timing mothers were also vocal regarding both advantages and disadvantages in timing the births of their children when they did. Many early-timers reported that because they had not established a definite lifestyle before parenthood, having a child proved less disruptive for them. This intrusion of a child on a previously established routine was an aspect of parenting that late-timers agreed was very difficult for them. In fact, late-timers perceived the initial adjustment to motherhood as more difficult for them than the early-timers did. Furthermore, the late-timers experienced an erosion of their self-confidence postmotherhood and greatly missed the verbal feedback and stimulation of a job during the earliest months of caring for their infants.

Early-timing mothers felt that they were more spontaneous toward life because they were younger. They considered this an advantage in that they could go with the flow of a household with younger children. A 24-year-old mother commented:

Parents who are older when they have their kids annoy me. They say "I'm going to have this first child to end all first children—this is the baby to end all babies. If I stay home with my child, I am the first person to do this the right way." I resent that. They do things by the book. "This is the biggest thing that happened in the world—I am going to buy the best crib." They are into baby technology—they think there is a right way to do babies. I fly by the seat of my pants—that's what they're [they late-timers] not prepared for.

Other early-timing mothers reported that their youth is an advantage for them as mothers because they tend to play more spontaneously with their children and are less goal-directed with their time. Indeed, many late-timing mothers reported that they found it difficult to play with their children but enjoyed more goal-directed activities. A 26-year-old mother with three young children said:

I had a girlfriend who had her first at forty when I had my first, and the kids were born on the same day—but she doesn't have time to sit down with her daughter and write words with her or play games with her. I sit down with my daughter and Linda can pick out words in the book, and Barbie can't because Donna is more into "I have to get the dishes done. I have to get the ironing done." She's used to doing that. At five years old, the kid is sitting there ironing clothes. I don't even do it. I think when you're older it's hard to break with that routine—you're used to a gorgeous house and you're set and then it's harder to let yourself go and say "Let them be." You are more into your career, and when you leave work it's more traumatic, and now some of us said we didn't care if we left our jobs. We're more contented—we're more easygoing. They're so used to having a clean house and spotless shirts that they can't relax. If the kids get sick on them, they're in heart failure. I can let the dishes pile up and I don't care. Plus, when you're in your twenties, the kids have friends and you get to meet the mothers—you get to have a social life.

It is significant that one of the disadvantages late-timers commented on was social isolation within their neighborhoods because of the lack of families with young children with whom these late-timers could socialize.

For other early-timing mothers, the advantage of timing children early in their twenties is having several years to enjoy their marital relationship once the children are grown. Late-timers agreed that they were concerned about being well into their fifties and having adolescent children intrude on their marriages. Early-timers also commented that there is an advantage to having children and parents grow up and struggle together—the children are not protected from seeing that life has its ups and downs. The lives of early-timing parents are not so smoothly designed in terms of career and family when their first children are born:

> We timed it to work out like this—both of us came from families where our fathers were in their late thirties. My husband's mother was forty—his father was a doctor and didn't have time for the kids—he didn't have time to grow up with them. My father was busy in his career, and my mother went out working when I was young. My father was sixty-five before my youngest brother hit eighteen. We wanted to have our children while we were young, before we were settled or entrenched in a career. And so that the kids would be grown up and on their own and we'd still have plenty of time for each other. I won't even be fifty when they're both out of college. We figure that will give us a lot of time to travel and do what we want. We decided, "Let's make things harder while we're younger when we're resilient and can handle things"—we think it's better for the kids—it gives them more time with us.

> I think it's been a good time to have kids, because my first child was born one month early—two weeks before my husband graduated from college—which was really close. Our son has really seen us struggle and have one career and grow to the maximum in that—grow toward another goal, reach that one, and start another. He's [her son] seen the whole process—he's been in on it. He's a really mature six-year-old because of it. We don't hide things from him—we discuss things in front of him. We may not include his opinion in our life goals, but he is aware that when we make big decisions we will sit and talk them over with him—when we're about to do something for what we've just completed. In that way, it really does give him a realistic picture of how one does have control and plan one's life.

Early-timers clearly felt disadvantaged in the area of finances and felt that this provided much less stability for them:

We had to borrow money from our parents to buy the house—we needed the money because we had a child. It seems like now that we have two children we never have any money—the paycheck comes in and goes out again. We're hoping in time that it will resolve itself in later years. I think if we had waited, we would have had money in the bank from full-time jobs.

When you have money problems, a little love goes out the window. I think we got it back, but we used to fight all the time just over money—that was the big disadvantage.

Having kids when we did—one of us has always worked, but never both of us. We never had the second paycheck to stick aside and build up anything—so I worked and put my husband through college the first time, and then he worked for a while and I took care of the two kids.

The reports from both early- and late-timing mothers suggest that they perceived both advantages and disadvantages to their choice of timing; yet most of the women were quite satisfied regarding their choice.

9

Parenthood: An Opportunity to Develop as an Adult

A LTHOUGH parenthood is viewed as one of the most crucial tasks of adult life, there is little understanding of how a woman's experience with motherhood affects her development as a person. The effects of mothers on children have been studied extensively, but the reverse effect of motherhood on women has not been fully explored.[1] If early- and late-timing mothers are so different in terms of how they view and experience motherhood might not the effect of motherhood on their personal development as women also vary?

Adult developmental theory indicates that, during their twenties, adults are shifting their "center of gravity" from their family of origin to their own home base, whereas during their thirties, adults are developing roots and "settling down."[2] Women who delay childbearing are choosing motherhood during a life phase when they are experiencing a more serious sense of commitment and responsibility. These women have already moved out of the phase in which the task is separating from parents and achieving a sense of competency. During the years that they are parenting young children, they are less vulnerable around issues of competency and separation but perhaps more vulnerable around issues of intimacy and taking care of others. Women who choose motherhood earlier in their adulthood are doing so at a time when adult life is more tentative and when possibilities for future commitment are being explored. These younger mothers are coping with the adult tasks of separation and achievement while they are struggling with the tensions of parenthood.

In general, I found that the lives of both early- and late-timing mothers are dramatically changed by their experience with motherhood. My research suggests that a woman experiences growth and development along with the growth and development of her child. This highlights the ongoing, reciprocal, interactive relationship between mother and child. However, the nature of this reported change or growth is significantly different for late-timing and early-timing mothers, as parenthood facilitates the woman's work on unfinished adult tasks.

Late-Timing Mothers Discover a More Emotional, Nurturing Aspect of Themselves

As noted earlier, once they have children, late-timing mothers are more interested in developing friendships than younger mothers are. This finding was surprising to me, but it is not so surprising when it is integrated with the fascinating responses from these women when they were invited to tell me (both on the questionnaire and during the group interviews) how motherhood had most changed their lives. As noted in chapter 7, many late-timers have chosen to remain at home with their children or to reprioritize their work lives by working part-time or by working more flexible hours that mesh with their new role as mothers. These women thoroughly enjoy the nurturing and care-giving aspects of parenthood. In fact, both the questionnaires and the group discussions suggest that, for the late-timing mother, parenthood evokes the emotional, warm, nurturing aspect of her personality. A mother who works full time as an accountant reported:

> Sometimes I have a hard time opening up and being warm. It's amazing since having a child how mushy and lovey and affectionate I am with my child. I never knew I had that stuff in me. It showed a whole different side of myself— actually helped me appreciate my parents more and helped me to break down barriers in having some difficulty showing emotions.

Similarly, a 33-year-old mother whose son is 6 months old reported that she experiences herself as a more open, softer person since moving away from a difficult work situation that tended to make her wear a "shell of armor":

> You know, I think Martin has really done me a lot of good in that the last couple of years before he came along I was in a work situation that was real hard—it was unsafe in a lot of ways—a lot of anxiety and a lot of political infighting. I and others who worked there had to put shells on in order to survive and be safe. Martin really softened me up. . . . I had forgotten in some ways how to be as open as I want to be. Having him really helped me reconnect with that ability, and I didn't realize that. After he came, I didn't realize that I

had created such a hard shell for myself in this work situation. I feel almost relieved that I don't have to wear that shell anymore, and I don't feel like I do. It's very safe to be real open.

Both of these late-timing mothers seem to be saying that motherhood has enabled them to break down emotional barriers, thereby helping them become more open and more able to relate to others.

Most of the older mothers had chosen to work out a sense of self before motherhood—through work, career, or some other outside interest. The experience of motherhood has moved them from this more achievement- or goal-oriented focus to a lifestyle centered on their relationships with others. Many late-timing mothers, in responding to their child's emotional needs, discover a nurturing side of themselves that they did not even know existed before they became mothers. It is almost as though motherhood has released a relationship-oriented potential or a new capacity and desire for intimacy within their lives. A 37-year-old mother with two preschool-aged sons reported this identity change following motherhood:

I have two children and I'm expecting a third. David is four and Paul is two—I was a teacher before David was born. I never did go back to that. I did work on a part-time basis once per week while David was still young. The one thing that really impresses me is that while we all have motherhood as a common factor . . . after becoming a mother you identify yourself as being a mother first—motherhood pulls you into all sorts of activities and friends that you never would have been in necessarily.

Mothers who delay childbearing feel that motherhood "allows" them to experience relationships with more intensity. As one mother poignantly put it:

I don't know whether my capacity has grown more intense or whether I've gotten in touch with something that was already there—but I feel so much more intensity about how I feel toward my children and that spills over into everything you do—what I do outside the home and my relationship with my husband. Everything just seems so much more intense to me.

One late-timing mother said that teaching was much easier once she became a mother because of a change in her perceptions:

One thing that's really marvelous is that I've always been meant to have this role, but I've never put it on myself to really live it. I'm teaching art, and the students obviously want all this mothering—it used to annoy me so much when they'd come up and tell me their problems. I said that they'd just have to get it together, as that is the important thing around here. And even after I was pregnant with Laura, it was much easier and the classes were much more fun—I was willing to let them be babies and just mother them. . . . [Now] it's really all right with me if they want to be babies and give them a little pat on the head.

Another mother summed it up:

I didn't know I was capable of feeling such an unconditional love for another person. This [motherhood] has improved my relationship with my husband, my parents, and my in-laws.

Iris Kern reported that the reason the late-timers she interviewed had given up "$40,000 to $50,000 jobs with little or no regret in order to raise children" was that their values had changed. What these women wanted at this stage of life was to do something entirely different from making money, or what had previously been defined as "the productive, achievement oriented life."[3]

During one of my interviews, a 36-year-old mother who has a 2-year-old daughter expressed her sentiments in this regard:

It's changed me a lot [having a child], in that I don't take life in a five-year plan—or in semesters—it just has really slowed me down a lot. Which is nice—to live for the moment. I don't think I've ever had the luxury of being able to do that before. You really have to do it with children, because you never know what's going to happen in the next minute. I do wonder how people can capsulize their life and get their kid off to the babysitter by 7:45. Those people do have a firmer grip on the hours—therefore it's got to be on the retirement plans and five years from now—it all works hand in hand. But that's something that's really changed for me—because I was always that kind of person—I wanted to know what I had achieved. I would have wanted to be sure that I was headed on an exact radar—from the time I was fifteen I was goal-oriented, and you really can't be as goal-oriented with a very young child.

Motherhood seems to push late-timers to slow down and enjoy their lives—to be less goal-oriented and more spontaneous. Many of them expressed extreme satisfaction with this new life-style. In response to a comment by one mother who said she found great pleasure in "seeing the world again through the eyes of a child," another late-timing mother, who is employed part-time, commented on how motherhood pushes her to enjoy herself more than she did before:

> You put it in different words, but what I was thinking was that motherhood forces me to take the time that I would like to do anyway. I do art work professionally – I'm a fairly creative person, but I don't ever do that at home on my own. . . . I find it [motherhood] forces me to do little creative things that I really enjoy doing for myself but that I didn't do until she came along and gave me a really good reason to do them. I had a good time with her Halloween costume this year. I'm the kind of person that has to be forced to take the time to do those things that I enjoy.

These themes that emerged during the group discussions are further corroborated by a content analysis of responses to an open-ended question on the questionnaire, which invited participants to note the ways in which they have changed most significantly since becoming mothers. The responses of the late-timing mothers cluster around two main topics. Thirty-one percent of the responses cluster around the theme of having "given up a career, work, freedom or time for self." This cluster of responses corroborates findings that have been reported in earlier chapters regarding the late-timer's ability to recognize and find ways to meet her own needs as well as those of her children.

However, almost half of the responses indicate that motherhood has added a new dimension to the lives of these women, enabling them to feel more loving and connected to the rest of the world. A 31-year-old woman who is the mother of a 6-month-old daughter commented as follows:

> It [motherhood] has added a new dimension. I think I am more loving and accepting and less selfish a person. On a practical level – I am for the first time being at home and not actively involved in my career – a major change.

A 39-year-old mother who has two children, aged 5 and 18 months, agreed:

> [Motherhood] has given me the opportunity to experience a very unique love relationship. It has made me more flexible and more self-aware.

A 35-year-old mother who has a 4-year-old daughter summed it up very well when she noted the most significant way in which parenthood has changed her life:

> Intensity and understanding and depth of feeling. All things we thought we understood before but had only just begun. All of these apply personally to

relationships with our parents, between my husband and myself and to more general things, like relating to books and other people's problems, joys, and tragedies.

Parenthood appears to increase the late-timing mother's capacity for understanding and experiencing her emotions and to facilitate an intense focus on relationships with others. This focus may have been neglected when these women were establishing career or work interests during their twenties.

As noted earlier, late-timers reported that friendships with other women became significantly more important to them after they became mothers. Furthermore, most women who delayed childbirth elected to spend a large portion of their time at home with their preschool children. When late-timers returned to work, it was most often on a part-time basis. The development of friendships and taking care of children are expressions of engaging in relationships with others, so perhaps this shift in the personal development of late-timing mothers provides a partial explanation for these findings.

Early-Timing Mothers Become More Responsible and Autonomous

During group discussions early-timers described motherhood as an opportunity to grow and develop in concert with their children. As one 23-year-old mother commented:

> Maybe the way you look at it changes as you go through different stages—like *Passages*. Right now all I see myself as is the mother of two young children. I don't see myself as wife before the children. . . . I think it must change every few years—your life changes as the children grow—you change all the time.

As a result of motherhood, early-timing mothers learn to be more independent, to set clearer priorities, and to find out who they are. Many young mothers remarked that they had become more responsible, more self-disciplined, and more self-assured since becoming mothers. A 24-year-old mother, who has two preschool-aged children, commented:

> I think I've become more self-disciplined since I'm a mother. I mean, here you are in charge of a house and kids and now I have to organize in order to get everything done. You're in charge and you have to get it done.

For early-timing mothers, parenthood is being a responsible, mature, self-confident adult—in short, growing up. During a small-group discussion, one early-timing mother remarked:

I think I've taken more responsibility on myself and trust my intuition more since I became a mother.

The small-group discussions revealed that women who had timed the birth of their first children fairly early in their adult life felt more self-assured and more mature in their new role as mother. One young mother said, "When you're the mother, you're not the kid anymore." These women saw themselves as taking on more responsibility, becoming more self-disciplined, and feeling good about growing with their children. Many agreed that motherhood had been an integral part of their adult development. Two young mothers commented that motherhood enhanced their feelings of self-confidence and trust in their own judgments and opinions:

I think I'm more self-assured. I feel like I can handle a lot of situations now. I used to have a thing about being afraid of older people—like they knew every-thing. Now I think that I've been around the block a few times and I knew a few things. . . . When I was in the hospital with my son he had a lot of colic—I was wondering if it was a milk allergy—he was on a formula. I would read about it and suggest it to my pediatrician and he said, "No, this kid is fine," and proceeded to denigrate me as a mother. . . . I kept saying there was something wrong with this child. . . . Finally, I said, "I don't have to listen to him—I can do something else." On my own, I switched to a soybean formula and saw another pediatrician. This new pediatrician said "Yes, you were absolutely right—it is a milk allergy." I thought "Well, if I figured this out, I can do a lot of other things myself."

I'm much more responsible. My parents are amazed that I've taken on this responsibility. I make decisions and I am much more self-confident. I inter-viewed pediatricians. I didn't know anything about them—I guess I was intimi-dated by people. Before I was a mother, if I was on a committee, somebody would shoot me down, and now I just say how I feel. I accept feedback, but I was never so bold before. Now I say what I think.

This same tendency appears in the questionnaire data regarding how motherhood had most changed the women's lives. Responses clustered around two main themes: "having become more responsible or serious as a person" (26 percent) and "feeling very full and complete" (21 percent). One early-timing mother commented:

It's forced me to be more aware of my surroundings and to become more asser-tive, to grow up—to be able to look at life in a very different way.

This tendency to feel more responsible and autonomous following parenthood is very different from the feelings of the late-timers, who reported that parenthood intensified and deepened their emotional life and improved their relationships with others. This feeling of responsibility was expressed in different words by two other early-timing mothers, aged 25 and 24 respectively:

> Motherhood helps me have more responsibility — helps me have better priorities.

> Being responsible physically, emotionally, and mentally for the development of another person — I have become much more serious about life.

Perhaps, for women who time their first births early in their twenties, motherhood has more influence in shaping their less well developed sense of identity by providing them with a sense of purpose. Furthermore, parenthood may provide these women with an extra push to work on the unfinished adult task of separation from family of origin while they are creating a new family with their husbands and children.

Self-Esteem

There appears to be some conflict in the literature about the effects of motherhood on the self-esteem of adult women. Some researchers believe that the birth of their first child is the greatest developmental crisis a women faces during her lifetime. For Therese Benedek, the "integrative task of pregnancy and motherhood" is biologically, psychologically, and realistically a much greater task than a woman has previously faced.[4] Judith Bardwick noted that, for most women, motherhood looms as a critical life task, because the culture defines it as an important symbol of normality and maturity. Motherhood gives a woman a feeling of "having achieved adult status and of having joined the community of adult women." In addition, it provides a "criterion for self-esteem" and it is one route to identity and a "lifetime of defined behaviors."[5] For the early-timing mothers in my study, motherhood indeed seems to provide them with a symbol of maturity, responsibility, and an adult status.

Despite the difficulty of the transition to parenthood, both Therese Benedek and Margaret Mahler have been optimistic about the effects of motherhood on a woman's life. They have emphasized that in each critical period of child development, the child revives in the parent his or her own related developmental conflicts from childhood. Although there is a possibility of pathological development in the parent, there is also a potential for achieving new levels of integration upon resolution of the conflict from the parent's own past life.[6]

Alice Rossi has been more pessimistic about the effect of parenthood on women's lives. She has pointed to research demonstrating that the transition to parenthood is not necessarily positive for women. Rossi believes there is ample evidence that, for many women, maternity has not provided opportunities for personal growth and development. For many women whose interests and values enabled them to combine work and marriage successfully, the addition of maternal responsibilities leads to a "fundamental and undesired change in both their relationships to their husbands and their involvements outside the family." For other women, the reactivation of older, unresolved conflicts with their own mothers is "not favorably resolved" and leads to "personality deterioration" and to resulting problems with their children. Rossi has claimed that if these women had not become mothers, they might have been able to sustain more adequate functioning as adults.[7]

Motherhood has also been described as "an ambivalent role—a curtailment of one's lifestyle." For the woman who has evolved a sense of self that includes being involved with the "outer world," the new world of being at home with young children may be threatening to her self-esteem and self-concept. This career-oriented woman "may ask what she has become, who she is, what she has done with her potential." She may become threatened because her image of herself was as an achievement-oriented, self-directed, independent woman.[8] The data from my study regarding attitudes toward work and motherhood suggest that although the late-timing mother who has been independent and achievement-oriented may have some initial doubts about herself in this new role, she experiences joy and a sense of enrichment from the opportunity to nurture a child.

Other data contradict some of these findings, however, and indicate some areas of insecurity for the late-timing mother in her new role of parent. When asked the degree to which their experience as a mother has increased or decreased their positive feelings regarding themselves, early-timing mothers perceived a significantly ($p < 0.5$) higher increase in the positive effects of motherhood on their self-esteem.[9] In fact, there is a very high positive correlation ($r = .7485$) between age and self-esteem, suggesting that the younger the mother, the more she feels that motherhood has increased her self-esteem.

Late-timing mothers have developed more of a sense of themselves before becoming parents and find the experience of motherhood more disruptive to their ongoing lives. Also, women who delay childbirth, because they are closer to 40 when they are parenting young children, are closer to examining the issue of morality and to understanding a different foundation for their self-esteem. Perhaps they have begun to realize that self-esteem cannot emanate solely from an external role but must depend on an inner core of contentment and acceptance of oneself.

In support of these statistical findings, it is significant that, during the group discussions, several late-timing mothers reported that they felt less confident in themselves since becoming mothers. One mother spoke movingly about the erosion of her self-confidence following the birth of her first child:

> I feel that I've become more indecisive—when I had a job and responsibility and was in charge of certain things and had authority and knew this had to be done—and could tell so-and-so to do that—I had a good deal of confidence. I had feedback from people too—you always hear, when you have a job, whether or not you've done that job all right. Whereas, in being a mother I feel that I have a little bit less self-confidence—I'm not having a review of my job.

This comment struck some responsive chords among the other women in that discussion group. Other late-timing mothers added their own concerns about their lack of self-esteem when they do not receive feedback from a more structured job outside the home. A 36-year-old mother asked the woman who commented about "not having a review of my job":

> Do you mean self confidence about reentering the working world?

The woman responded:

> No—I mean about being a mother. Also, I don't know why, but I also seem to be more indecisive. Maybe it's the lack of confidence that makes me indecisive—about whether I'm going to do one thing or another. Whereas, when I had a job I was not [indecisive].

Another mother spoke of feeling "fragmented," and others noted feelings of frustration in not experiencing a sense of accomplishment when they stay home with their children:

> My image of myself has dissolved a bit or has become a little foggier—fuzzy around the edges.

When I was on my maternity leave, my husband would come home at the end of the day and he'd say, "What did you do?" At my job I work on a 24-hour cycle—I'd work on something and then it's on the air and it's done and you could look at it. You could see it.

There was a certain frustration for me [in being home]—there was not a tangible thing. I felt like what I was doing was very important, but it didn't sound very impressive to anybody and it didn't sound as though it could ever fill the whole day.

Yes, like I did six loads of laundry today.

Plus, the results of all your efforts will not bring you fruit for a number of years.

Comments like these were rarely voiced by early-timing mothers, who had not defined themselves in terms of the work world before becoming mothers. Yet early-timers are also struggling with identity problems, because they have derived their self-esteem and sense of who they are from external others. However, they may experience less discomfort when they become mothers, because they have not moved beyond early adulthood and have not yet begun to question themselves and the meaning of life in the same way late-timing mothers have.

Two late-timing mothers discussed the advantages of returning to school on a part-time basis as a way of coping with this worry about losing one's self-confidence:

I'm just curious, Pamela—having been at home with children and now going back to school to get a degree—which I might be interested in doing—how has your idea of yourself changed?

You mean about my self-confidence? I feel that I've lost confidence in myself staying at home—I've lost confidence in myself as far as returning to the working world. With each year that I'm home, I feel a little less confident about getting back there.

I would agree with that. Now, taking courses, do you feel differently?

No, because I'm still not out there. . . . [School is] a very unrealistic world.

But you're accomplishing something specific.

Yes, but I'm still not out there. I haven't established that confidence yet. With each year that I stay home, I lose a little more confidence about reentering the working world—whatever it might be.

I think I have a lot of that too. I haven't been [away from work] that long, but I worked for a bank. I still have a lot of friends who are in banking, and once in awhile we'll talk about banking. I'll say, "Oh, my God, I'm really slipping—I don't know about that—what's it going to be like in several years when I go back into it?" Then I start thinking I can't go back into that because I'll never be sharp enough—I'll have to pick something else. You really do lose your self-confidence in a very short time.

School keeps my self-confidence—it keeps my mind sharp. For me, it's the one thing that I feel that I'm doing for myself that makes me feel good about me—just for me—not for my husband and not for my child—it's for me. It's helped me to maintain my confidence. On the other hand, I've lost [self-confidence] in another area.

Finally, a 38-year-old mother summed up the feelings and attitudes of these women very well:

One area that I think I've really changed—I came from before having babies to a job that was so scheduled—I had dates to remember—programs to get out—I was very regimented—and I can't seem to finish a project now. I can't get a job done. I think this bothers me an awful lot. My mind has ten different things going at one time—if I could only figure how I'm going to get project number 1 done before I go to project number 2 when ten of them need attention.

Late-timers, though satisfied as mothers, are also frustrated with the lack of feedback and the lack of an opportunity to set goals and experience a sense of completion on a task. This frustration may relate to their comments regarding a certain "fuzziness" about their identity and to their lower scores on the scale indicating the degree to which motherhood has increased their self-esteem. Often, activities that produce the highest level of satisfaction may also produce more internal conflict and stress—just as activities that are not highly rewarding may also not be stressful. For example, studies have indicated that, for most adults, marriage and parenthood provide the greatest source of both satisfaction and anxiety.[10]

These findings regarding self-esteem suggest that late-timers may be experiencing a transition in the source of feedback for their self-esteem. As mothers, they are forced to examine themselves and determine who they are with or without a work role. They may be approaching an understanding that the best source of self-esteem is an internal one. Struggling with feeling "fuzzy around the edges" may represent an important growing edge for these mothers who spent their twenties receiving strokes from their work outside the home.

Adjustment to Parenthood

A search of the literature on the timing of parenthood reveals that most researchers and popular writers agree with Foltz's findings:

> Late-timing parents have resolved major identity, work and intimacy issues which allowed them to enjoy their new status as parents with less conflict than those parents who entered parenthood still in the midst of substantial struggles to establish intimacy, identity and a career.[11]

However, much of the research and some of the popular articles also indicate that women who had their first children in their late twenties or early thirties found adjustment to parenthood more difficult than those who timed their first children early in their twenties. Daniels and Weingarten found this to be true, as did Rossi in her pilot study on the meaning of age and aging in relationship to parenting and the psychological well-being of women in the middle years. The results of Rossi's study suggest that having children at an older age is related to greater child-rearing difficulties than having a first birth early in one's adult life. Rossi's data also suggest that this is true for coping with infants, preschoolers, and older adolescents. In analyzing the woman's relationship to her early adolescent child, for example, Rossi found:

> The older the mother, the more she reports the child is critical of her, the less sociable the child is and the less emotional closeness there is in the mother–child relationship.[12]

The trends in the data suggest that, to cope with their own aging process, women may tend to turn inward and be less emotionally available to their children.

Naomi Munson found that women who have delayed childbirth have been in the habit of doing things for themselves:

> [They] are determined to see the process through in a rational and intelligent manner — unlike their own mother who plunged unthinkingly into the pro-

creative cycle. And they are also determined that pregnancy and motherhood will not interfere with whatever else they have chosen to do with their lives.[13]

Thus, although postponement of the first birth may be helpful in their efforts to complete professional training or to become more established in a meaningful job or career, there are likely to be some unanticipated difficulties in the child-rearing role for women who delay childbearing into their thirties.

When asked to describe their personality characteristics on an adjective checklist, the late-timing mothers in my study perceived themselves as significantly ($p < .10$) more unsure, anxious, self-doubting, confused, and conflict-laden than the early-timing mothers did. Furthermore, scores on a scale measuring adjustment to motherhood indicated that late-timers had significantly more difficulty adjusting to motherhood ($p < .07$). As noted earlier, late-timers tend to plan, structure, and order their lives to a greater extent than early-timers do, and the arrival of a child may cause more disruption in a woman's life when she has such a strong need for structure and organization. Late-timers expressed some anxiety regarding the earliest stages of motherhood—when the need for adjustment is critical. For example, one late-timing mother said:

> Do you think as older parents we are more worried about consequence—for instance, stimulating your baby enough? When you were describing your mother, who had her children earlier, she seemed to be much more relaxed. I have a suspicion—I can think back to the anxiety of having Samantha as a tiny baby at home—and yet I can think, "Of course, you can handle this infant baby."

Another woman, who was 33 when her first child was born, said:

> I agree. I was in the hospital having just produced my first child and looked at it—her—and the little crib thing lying next to my bed and I didn't know how to pick her up. How do I pick her up? She's so floppy—my mom came in and slid her hand under her head and I was fascinated because I'd been too scared to do it.

One late-timer reported that her pediatrician had commented:

> You older mothers—you've been working or doing something in a situation where you've been in control—you know what to do to fix this or that—then

this little person comes along who doesn't only not wear a watch, but doesn't know all this kind of stuff.

Summary

It appears that late-timing mothers perceive the initial adjustment to motherhood to be more difficult. For women who delay childbearing, motherhood represents a very different lifestyle from the experience of working outside the home in a job where positive feedback is more readily available. Late-timers (particularly if they do not return to work on a full-time basis) are forced to examine who they are in a critically different way. The recognition they received from their role as "competent worker" can no longer sustain or support their self-esteem as it once did, and they're having to look inside themselves for a source of support. Furthermore, late-timers, by virtue of their maturity and education, seem to be more concerned about their own behavior. This may explain their perception of themselves as unsure, self-doubting, and anxious.

Also, new mothers must be more able to go with the flow of daily activity, rather than adopting an orderly schedule, which is more often the style adopted in work life outside the home. Planning and organization of their daily lives is the preferred style of the late-timing mothers interviewed in this study. Thus, the most difficult period of parenting for late-timers may be the earliest months of parenthood, when the need to go with the flow of daily activity is greatest.

For early-timing mothers, parenthood has effected global changes in their development. In a sense, they have grown up as a result of motherhood. They experience more autonomy and feel that parenthood provides them an opportunity to grow and develop along with their children. Early-timing mothers seem more merged with their children from birth and use the mother-child matrix as a way to differentiate themselves and to separate themselves from their own parents. For these young women, the task of early adulthood—separation and individuation—is being accomplished through motherhood. Parenthood seems to push these women toward a more responsible, mature style of behavior. This may help to explain why, following motherhood, self-esteem scores are increased for early-timing mothers at a more significant level than for late-timing mothers.

Late-timing mothers have chosen to establish a sense of identity before motherhood, via work, career, or some other outside interest. The task of their twenties—separation from their home base and development of a sense of competency—has been accomplished through work or career. Choosing parenthood in their thirties facilitates moving from this more autonomous style to a focus that includes both achievement and caring for others. Thus, motherhood has enabled these women to work on the adult tasks of intimacy and generativity. Women who enjoyed their work or careers for several years before motherhood are enthralled with motherhood and are pleased that it has pushed them to invest more in other relationships, such as their marriages and friendships with other women.

Parenthood has thus had a powerful impact on the lives of both early- and late-timing mothers. Childbirth acts as a catalyst for adult growth by intensifying the shift in a direction in which the adult is already propelled. Whatever the timing, parenthood looms as a powerful "mover and shaker." The findings of my study support theories that suggest the possibility for "achievement of new levels of integration" following parenthood.[14] Yet parenthood does more than help resolve old conflicts from childhood; it also pushes a woman to work more intensely on her current adult life tasks and areas of vulnerability. The early-timers were pushed to work hard on separation/individuation, whereas the late-timers were working on intimacy issues, having achieved a sense of autonomy through their careers during their twenties.

There are clear indications that parenthood is a developmental, reciprocal process that catches the woman and engages her in caring for another human being. Simultaneously, parenthood also facilitates the growth and development of the less well developed side of the woman's personality.

10

Conclusions

MOTHERHOOD is one of the most challenging developmental tasks a woman faces during her lifetime. When a woman becomes a mother, she must adjust to significant changes in her view of herself, her role in her marriage, her body, and her place in the larger context of the outside world. Furthermore, she must adjust and react to a newly created intimate relationship with her child. Because the child is constantly changing and growing, the mother must react to a situation that is in almost constant flux. The effect of the child's growth on the mother and the effect of the mother's growth on the child is an exciting, interactive phenomenon.

Parenthood provides an opportunity for growth and development as an adult. The experience of parenthood is a reflection of an adult's struggle with the two basic tensions in life: autonomy—taking care of oneself and tuning in to one's own needs; and homonomy—relating to and taking care of others. Thus, the tensions of parenthood mirror the larger tensions of life with which every adult must struggle. Specifically, motherhood requires that a woman cope with merging and separation. As the child moves from needing a closely attached, symbiotic relationship with the mother to needing more distance and a chance to develop his or her own personality, the mother must respond in different ways. This can affect her daily functioning and whether she does or does not fulfill her own emotional needs.

The mothers who shared their experiences in this book informed us that motherhood, whatever the timing, can be both gratifying and frustrating. The most gratifying experiences provide the mother with an opportunity to integrate and consolidate what she has learned. For example, late-timing mothers find watching their child's development most exciting. They have moved out of their twenties and have focused on the adult task of separation from their families to achieve a sense of autonomy. They now seize the opportunity to integrate this experience as they parent their preschool children.

The tensions of parenthood also signify a "growing edge" for adults. The frustrations of parenthood may provide a woman with an opportunity to develop an aspect of her personality that is as yet unexplored and may represent an arena in which she may be most vulnerable. For example, what is most difficult for an early-timing mother is physical and emotional separation from her child, because she herself is struggling with separation and individuation in her adult life. Thus, the timing of parenthood has a potentially positive impact for all women, regardless of whether the birth of the first child occurs early or later in adulthood. Parenthood challenges a woman to cope with inner tensions (with which she may already be struggling) in a very intense way.

The Importance of Taking Care of Yourself and Your Child

One important message from the mothers featured in this book is that a woman doesn't have to be "all mother" to be a "good enough mother." One of the most difficult aspects of motherhood for all women—regardless of the timing—seems to be balancing their personal needs for space and sense of self with the emotional demands that a preschool child places on a mother. The mothers in this study revealed that if a woman waits until her thirties to have her first child, she is more likely to nurture both herself and her child. The late-timer is more likely to say to herself, "I can take care of myself and my child."

The data seem to indicate that those women who have delayed childbirth until age 30 or later may be especially appreciative of the positive aspects of mothering and yet may be more able to cope with the frustrating parts. They enjoy nurturing the child during infancy and can also accept and cope with the child's need for distance and separation after the first year of life. Indeed, they seem to be intrigued with the spirit of their young children as they press for independence. These women have had the advantage of several years of adult development, during which they have worked on creating a personal sense of identity that emanates from their own ability to achieve or create or simply survive on their own.

Women who have timed motherhood earlier in their lives (late teens or early twenties) have not had the same time to explore who they are without an integral attachment to their husbands, children, and parents. Their identity is very tied up with their relationships with these important others. Although the early-timing mothers enjoy nurturing their children and being emotionally attached to them, they reported discomfort and frustration when their children begin to ask for distance and separation within the mother–child relationship. The child's need for discipline requires that the mother separate herself emotionally from her child, and this is the most difficult aspect of parenting for the early-timing mother.

Although all the women who participated in this study seemed to have made fairly good adjustments to their role as mothers, there appeared to be more frustration and anger among the early-timing mothers. This anger may stem from a feeling of having lost touch with who they are—apart from their identity as mother of their children. When the boundary between parent and child is very weak and the parent is unsure of who is who, anger and frustration can build over time.[1] It is easier for a woman to cope with significant changes in her body, her identity, and her roles and relationships with others (including her child as he or she develops) when she is more certain of who she is before this drastic change. Late-timing mothers seemed able to retain this sense of self when they merged with their infants during the early months of life and again in later months, when developing children strike out for greater independence.

Aggressive Strivings and the Capacity for Dependency Are Important Components of Motherhood

The reports from the late-timing mothers provide a challenge to some of the traditional literature, which supports the idea that becoming an adequate mother requires comfort with a passive process within oneself—almost a negation of the more aggressive, achievement-oriented strivings. Several theorists have indicated that career-oriented women, or women "with other interests," would have difficulty opening themselves up enough to allow a child to be appropriately dependent on them.[2] I found, however, that women who had delayed parenthood expressed comfort in coping with their children's dual needs for closeness and attachment to the mother as well as distance and separation from the mother. These mothers also encouraged their children's development of their own independent style of functioning. In effect, these mothers were capable of moving in and out of a very emotionally and physically intimate relationship with their children as the children's needs for a certain kind of relationship changed.

One of the reasons for this comfort may be the late-timer's ability to accept and balance her own strivings and needs for affiliation (closeness) and achievement. Thus, some aggression complements the mothering process, particularly as it helps a mother become actively aware of and capable of meeting her own emotional needs while attending to the emotional needs of her child. The aggression of the late-timing mother enables her to define her own desires more clearly and to make some demands on her environment so that these needs are met. This is particularly true with regard to a desire for space and time for herself. By nurturing or taking care of herself, a woman has more emotional energy to offer her child.

Before becoming a parent, the late-timing mother has had more experience in caring for herself. Furthermore, the late-timer is more comfortable spending time alone. She has developed the capacity to count on herself and enjoys doing so. My research has indicated that the early-timing mother is much less comfortable spending time alone and may indeed be frightened at the prospect of having to count on herself for decision making. These younger women have had little time for personal development, as they have taken on marriage and motherhood before learning how to survive on their own. The early-timing mother becomes enmeshed in motherhood before she defines who she is and what she needs for herself. I was amazed at how many early-timing mothers were unaware that they might have needs of their own. Furthermore, the early-timers who were aware of wanting time for themselves were extremely frustrated because they were unable to find a way to get some personal space. Perhaps these younger women were also unsure about what they might do with personal time and space if it were available to them.

One of the striking findings of my research was that late-timing mothers reported greater comfort with their own dependency needs. These mothers were able to ask for help from others (husbands and friends) when they needed it, particularly in regard to the tensions of child rearing. They have developed the capacity to rely on themselves, yet they can also depend on others, when necessary, to meet some of their emotional needs.

Consequently, late-timers tend to recognize their own need for some personal space when confronted with the overwhelming needs of an infant or a preschool child. They are able to ask for and receive the emotional support they need. They appear to be more satisfied with their role as mothers than early-timers, who have not yet balanced this self–other tension.

On the personality inventory, early-timing mothers described themselves as subservient and dependent on others. However, they may not accept this part of themselves. Early-timers may be more conflicted with dependency than I had originally suspected. During discussions with early-timing mothers, the theme most frequently expressed was "need for control over my life." One mother, who was 23 when her first child was born, commented:

> I get pulled into things without trying. I have a hard time saying no. I overprogram myself and feel like my year is planned for me.

Perhaps lack of control over her life makes a woman less able to cope with intimacy and dependency in her life. When a woman's primary source of nourishment is external, there is little intrinsic reward for what she does. People who believe that everything they do is in response to the needs of others reduce the possibilities of making a meaningful contact with their environment and have difficulty with dependency issues.[3] Furthermore, early-timers have not fully developed the capacity to trust themselves and may be overwhelmed by their need for help from others—a need that seems so intense during the early years of parenting a small child.

Late-timing mothers have developed an identity based more on their own accomplishments and tend to use internal resources for daily decision making. These women feel more in charge of their lives and are less conflicted around dependency issues. Thus, I agree with Benedek, Grossman, and others that recognition and comfort with her own dependency needs is critical for a mother. However, from my research, I suggest that the more aggressive or achievement-oriented strivings inherent in the style of the late-timing mothers do not conflict with but rather complement and enhance the passive or more dependent tendencies that are also important in the mothering role. Just as the balancing of homonomous and autonomous strivings is important to our mental health, this balancing is crucial when mothering a preschool child.

Motherhood Facilitates the Completion of Unfinished Psychological Tasks

It seems clear that when early- and late-timing mothers begin the process of mothering, they have unfinished tasks to accomplish with regard to their own personal development. Research on women's lives has indicated that during their transition into early adulthood, women choose primarily affiliative or achievement-oriented paths. That is, most women choose either a career path or one that focuses more on homemaking and motherhood.

Toward age 30 or during their thirties, many women attempt to achieve a greater integration or balance between affiliation and achievement.[4]

The central task of the thirties is to balance needs that have formerly been perceived as oppositional to one another. A woman who has spent her twenties focusing primarily on her home and her relationships with her husband and children may want to try her hand at creating a more autonomous identity by entering the work force or by establishing creative outlets that provide another source of stimulation. On the other hand, a woman who has spent her twenties establishing a career focus may choose to explore the more affiliative or relationship-oriented aspect of her personality during her thirties.

A woman who times the birth of her first child in her thirties, when she is integrating affiliative and achievement needs, may have an advantage by virtue of her age. The personality inventory indicated that the late-timing mother perceived herself as submissive and nurturing and as striving for achievement and autonomy. Because she is tuned in to both aspects of her own functioning, the late-timer may be able to cope more successfully with a relationship to a preschool child, which is characterized by intermittent demands for closeness and distancing. Because the mother values her autonomy, the child's move toward independence can be viewed as a gain for both the mother and child, rather than as a loss for the mother.

For a woman who times the birth of her first child during her early twenties, affiliative and achievement needs are still very oppositional. The early-timer has not had an opportunity to begin work on balancing or integrating these needs. She has developed only the relational aspect of her personality and has not yet explored or integrated the achievement-oriented or autonomous aspect of her functioning. This younger woman may perceive her child's move toward independence as frightening, because her own identity is so intertwined with that of her child. She may fear that this reaching out by the child will break up a close-knit mother–child relationship, upon which the family system has been created.

It is significant, however, that women who are much younger when their first children are born experience themselves as becoming more autonomous, independent, and responsible as a result of parenthood. If I had an opportunity to interview these same young mothers again in their early to middle thirties, I suspect many of them would be completing their education or working in careers or jobs that interest them. During their thirties, these early-timing mothers may continue to foster the less developed aspect of their personality by choosing a more autonomous, independent focus. Although parenthood does not determine the course of adult development, it may serve as a catalyst, leading a woman in a direction that will enhance her personal growth. Because of the interrelationship of the timing of parenthood and other important demographic variables, such as education and family income, it is difficult to determine how powerful timing is in shaping development (see appendix).

Women Who Delay Childbearing Place a High Value on Relationships

The mothers in this study placed a high value on relationships in their lives. This finding supports Carol Gilligan's premise regarding the importance women place on relationships with others and caring for others. Most of the women who had delayed childbearing to establish a career decided either to stay home full time during the early years of their children's lives or to return to work on a part-time basis. Most of these mothers did not want their work outside the home to interfere with their relationships with their children.

It is significant that these women are not adopting a male model when coping with the work world; instead, they are finding ways to integrate family and career or other outside interests. Indeed, "a different voice" is being expressed by these late-timing mothers. Women who have been work-oriented before becoming mothers have decided that climbing the career ladder is not as important as being an integral part of their children's daily life. Although many of these women who have delayed childbearing want to stay involved with their work interests outside the home, they also want to remain at least as invested in their families. They seem to recognize that this decision may mean a detour in their chosen careers, but they are willing to take that risk for what they are giving and getting at home.

These late-timers are also getting in touch with the emotional, relational aspect of their personalities, which may have been more dormant in their twenties. The implications of the choices these women have made, as well as the ways in which motherhood has affected their functioning, are profound. Women who have children later, after developing a career, may want to help redesign the workplace so that it will accommodate the interests of both family and work. Instead of giving into the existing work structure erected by society, late-timers show signs of creating a new family–work arrangement that enables them to meet their needs for achievement and affiliation. Perhaps this model represents an optimistic trend for the future, in which an interest in relationships and family life can be valued as much as work and earning money. This indicator is especially hopeful in a society with a strong emphasis on competition within a capitalistic, profit-making structure.

Implications

The results of this exploratory study, which suggest that the personal development of mothers is closely related to their children's developmental achievements, point to the need for further efforts to increase society's understanding of the ways in which mothers change at each stage of their children's development.

This study also indicates a need for a follow-up examination of the lives of these early- and late-timing mothers five and ten years from now to understand how other stages of child development, such as adolescence, affect a woman's functioning. It would also be useful to interview these mothers in the future to understand how parenthood has continued to foster the integration of aspects of their personalities that they have not yet developed. Will the early-timer be working on integrating the autonomous side of her personality in her thirties? What will be the focus of the late-timing mother in her forties or fifties, when her preschooler is in school? Will work be more of a focus for her then than it was at the time of this study? The door is wide open for further study of the effects of parenthood on the lives of both men and women.

The results of this study have serious implications for our society and the way in which it still encourages women to become submissive to the needs of their preschool children. Although it is important to meet the needs of these young children, it is also crucial that women maintain a sense of their own identity and autonomy so that they can appropriately balance the distancing and merging required in their role as mothers. Mothers need to remember that they are people, too. They must recognize the importance of simultaneously meeting their own needs and those of their children. To be an effective parent, a woman does not have to be "all mother." In fact, women who recognize the importance of their commitment to themselves—apart from their role as parent—may be more satisfied with motherhood.

Regardless of the timing of parenthood in adult life, women find caring for preschool children challenging and frustrating. They all agree that having outside support available helps them function more effectively in this very demanding role. The woman who has delayed childbirth is breaking new ground in our society and does not have role models on which to base her actions or expectations. Furthermore, she is geographically and emotionally more distant from her extended family and from the neighborhood group as a source of support.

In my study, it was obvious that the small-group discussions provided these mothers with an opportunity to share experiences and exchange ideas—to serve as role models for one another. Community centers, churches, hospitals, day care centers, nursery schools, and other social service agencies must develop and continue to encourage the growth of support groups for mothers of young children. As the mothers who participated in my study can attest, sharing experiences with other women can be a valuable tool in coping with the tensions of parenthood.

Finally, parenthood facilitates personal growth for adults. The process of integrating self–other tensions in adult life parallels the mother's need to connect with and distance herself from her child. Parenthood may serve as a catalyst which leads an adult in a direction which will encourage the parent to work on unfinished tasks of adulthood. The women's voices heard in this book define the challenges, frustrations and rewards of motherhood. These voices may help to engender greater respect for the valuable role that mothers play in our society.

Appendix:

Study Population, Research Design, and Statistical Findings

The Mothers: Who Are They?

The women who participated in the study were all married and living at home with their husbands and children. Because I was primarily interested in experiences of women with preschool-aged children, all of the children were under 6 years of age. It was important that the women be not too far removed from easy recall of their early years of child rearing, and the age limit for the children also ensured that the early- and late-timing mothers were in a similar stage of parenthood.

When contacting possible volunteers for this study, I focused on a three-state area of the northeastern United States. Both urban and suburban women were included in the study, but no participants were from rural areas. For the group discussion method, it was important to find small groups of women who lived in the same general geographical area, so that the discussion could be held at a location convenient for all the women.

The participants were not selected randomly because of restrictions inherent in the characteristics of the population I was interested in studying. Thus, the extent to which results of this study may be generalized to a larger population is limited. With these limitations in mind, the reader can consider the findings as possible trends in what mothers are experiencing. It is significant, however, that some of the findings from this study have been verified by others in both professional and lay publications.[1]

The population was self-selected by a "snowballing method," whereby one person who is contacted provides names of other possible volunteers, who are contacted and asked for other names until the number of volunteers is reached. I also obtained names of women from other sources, including interested mothers who had heard about the study, pediatric nurses, nursing mothers' groups, and nursery schools. I then personally telephoned each woman and invited her to participate in one or both phases of the study.

In identifying the population for this study, there was no attempt to control for other intervening variables—such as the educational level or occupation of the mother, the number of children, or the family income—because it would have been impossible to obtain a sample if I had attempted to match the two groups on such variables when I suspected significant differences between them. Population statistics from the U.S. Census Bureau confirm that there are sharp differences between women who timed the birth of their first children before age 25 or after age 30 on various socioeconomic characteristics, such as family income, educational achievement, and occupation:

> Women thirty years and older in June 1982 who had their first birth in the previous month were more likely than eighteen to twenty-four year olds (the ages at which most first births typically occur) to have completed one year of college, to be employed and in a professional occupation and to live in families with relatively high incomes.[2]

The age at which a woman has her first child and other demographic variables—such as education, income, and occupation—are obviously interrelated in their effects on a woman's experiences with motherhood. This interrelationship among important variables limits the analysis, however, because it is difficult to determine the effect of any one variable.

Age

The early-timing mothers who participated in this study ranged in age from 19 to 25 at the time their first children were born, with an average age of 23. The women who had delayed childbirth were between 30 and 41 when they had their first children, with an average age of 32.

Number of Children

Sixty-four percent of the late-timing mothers had only one child, versus only 28 percent for the early-timers. Fifty-three percent of the early-timing mothers had two children, whereas only 28 percent of the late-timing mothers had two children—including one set of twins. Early-timers were also ahead with three-children families; 18 percent had three children, as opposed to only 5 percent (including a set of twins) for the late-timers.

On the average, the early-timing mothers had two children and the late-timers had one child. This factor may relate to the age of the late-timers, as they were older when they first gave birth and were very concerned about "being too old" to have another child. In addition, as the data disclosed, they plan to spend their time in other pursuits while they are mothers.

Education

Whereas 62 percent of the late-timers had graduate degrees, only 3 percent of the early-timers did. However, at the time of the study, several of the early-timers were working on advanced degrees in nursing and social work. This difference was expected, because the opportunity for further education and training beyond high school or college is one of the aspects of life that is relinquished by women who time the birth of their first children early in their twenties.

Nearly all late-timing mothers (97 percent) had earned college degrees; only 26 percent of the early-timing mothers had college degrees. It is significant, however, that 41 percent of the early-timing mothers had taken college courses for credit but had not yet earned degrees. Statistics from the U.S. Census Bureau corroborate my finding that late-timing mothers tend to achieve a higher level of education. According to population reports, "Seventy-eight percent of women thirty to forty-four years old who had a recent first birth had completed at least one year of college, compared with twenty-one percent of women eighteen to twenty-four years old."[3]

Socioeconomic Status

The late-timing mothers had more years of higher education, a higher socioeconomic status, and fewer children than the early-timers. However, the early-timing mothers comprised a very heterogeneous population. Their family incomes ranged from $15,000 to over $50,000 per year, with a median income between $25,000 and $35,000 per year, representative of a middle-income group. Their husbands' occupations ranged from semiskilled worker to professional.

Socioeconomically, the late-timing mothers were a more homogeneous group, with 80 percent of their family incomes over $35,000. Compared to the middle-income or lower-middle-income status of the early-timing group, the late-timing group can be described as having middle-income to upper-middle-income status. The average income for the late-timing group fell between $35,000 and $45,000 per year. As with the early-timing group, only a small percentage fell under $15,000 (5 percent). Again, statistics from the U.S. Census Bureau confirm these findings:

> A significantly higher proportion of women thirty years and older lived in families with incomes of $25,000 and over (fifty-five percent) than did those women who had their first birth at ages eighteen to twenty-four (seventeen percent).[4]

The women who participated in my study had higher family incomes than the average American family.

From an occupational perspective, the spouses of late-timing mothers also were a more homogeneous group than the spouses of the early-timing mothers. Of the late-timing husbands, 46 percent worked in professional occupations, such as medicine, law, psychology, and teaching, and 49 percent worked in managerial occupations, such as marketing, banking, planning, business, and management consulting.

Work Choices

The early- and late-timing mothers were in dissimilar occupations. Of the late-timing mothers who were employed at the time of the study, 40 percent were working in professions requiring several years of training, such as law, the ministry, and psychiatry. It is significant that none of the early-timing mothers were working in one of these professions. The remainder of the employed late-timing mothers were working in such occupations as social work, nursing, library science, financial analysis, management, writing, and interior design. Again, statistics from the U.S. Census Bureau confirm this difference:

> Among employed women, those aged thirty and over were more apt to hold a professional position (fifty-one percent) than were eighteen to twenty-four year olds (five percent).[5]

An equal percentage of late-timing mothers were full-time homemakers or working outside the home (46 percent); 7.7 percent were students. The breakdown for hours worked for the late-timing mothers who were working is as follows:

37–40 hours per week—24 percent

21–35 hours per week—35 percent

Fewer than 20 hours per week—41 percent

It is remarkable that although most late-timing mothers had worked for at least 6 years before the birth of their first child, less than 9 percent of the total group interviewed were currently working full-time (37–40 hours per week).

Since only about 25 percent of the early-timing mothers were working outside the home, the work statistics for them are insignificant—except that almost 90 percent of those who were employed were working part-time (fewer than 30 hours per week). Almost 70 percent of the early-timing mothers were full-time homemakers; 5 percent were students.

The work of the early-timing mothers clustered around semiprofessional (nursing, physical therapy) and clerical/sales positions. Again, as with the educational issue, this is not surprising when we consider that the late-timing mothers had more years for advanced training and had not put their careers "on hold" so that their husbands could advance in their careers, as many early-timing mothers had done.

The Study Design

Because of my interest in understanding how the experiences that women have as late-timing and early-timing mothers might be similar and different, I wanted to be certain to capture, insofar as possible, the actual thoughts and feelings these mothers were having at the time they participated in my study. My clinical group work with mothers of preschool-aged children, as well as my personal experiences as a mother and as a women, convinced me that one phase of the data collection had to include small-group discussions. In small groups, women could better share their thoughts and feelings about being a mother—including both the frustrations and the rewards of that role.

Small-Group Discussions

During any effectively facilitated group discussion, the responses of one person tend to build upon those of another because group participants often share material they might not have thought about individually. Small-group discussions provide a stimulating atmosphere for the emergence of issues and responses that are not tapped by individual questionnaires, thus adding to the intensity and richness of data collected on an individual basis. Moreover, the small-group discussions in this study provided an incentive for coming together as a group to share experiences regarding a very important role—being a mother. I believe that, when possible, clinical research should provide some personal benefit for the participants who so willingly share their lives with the researcher.

Throughout both phases of data collection, I received feedback from the women indicating that their participation in this research project helped them clarify their own perceptions and responses to motherhood. Some of these women felt that their lives had been changed in a positive direction by their participation in this research. This was particularly true in the small-group discussions, where they discovered both mutual support and a chance to air some differences in their experiences as women and as mothers. Many women exchanged phone numbers at the end of the discussion with the hope of establishing some new support networks.

It was gratifying to me that no mother who met the criteria for the study refused to participate in at least one phase of the study. In fact, from the time of my initial phone contacts with the mothers who agreed to participate, most women were extremely pleased that motherhood was being investigated in a systematic way. As one young mother said on the telephone:

> You mean you are really going to do a study about mothers and what they think? Gee, I think that is terrific. It makes me feel so important.

From my observations, these mothers sincerely wanted an opportunity to share their experiences with other mothers and wanted to alleviate the scarcity of information concerning the role of women as mother. These women were aware that American society places little economic and social value on this most difficult and vital role, and they felt that this study might help change that.

One limitation of the group method is the difficulty of data collection and analysis because of the complexity of interaction within the group. To deal with this complex observation and analysis of group data, a research assistant was hired to serve as a recorder and observer during each group session. Each session was preserved on audio tape so that transcripts could be prepared. Because the qualitative data from the transcripts are subjective, I also designed a method of organizing the data (content analysis) so that they could be appropriately coded and rated.[6]

Before submitting the tapes and transcripts to raters for analysis, a colleague and I listened to the tapes and transcripts to be certain that, within each group of responses following one of my questions to the group, the precoded response submitted to the raters was made by a different participant. In this way, a single, more vocal participant did not dominate the responses that were finally submitted to the raters.

I then developed a rating scheme so that two trained raters, who were blind to the design and assumptions of the research study, could independently evaluate the women's responses and determine whether there was sufficient agreement between the raters' observations on the rating scheme. This degree of agreement between two or more observers is known as *interrater reliability.*[7] Besides rating the group responses on a scheme, the two raters were also asked to describe, in a few paragraphs, the main themes that appeared to emerge regarding the meaning of motherhood for each group of women interviewed. These more global, subjective ratings were then compared with the more "biased" observations made by me and my research assistant.

Thus, all clinical observations and interpretations of what was said (content) and what occurred (process) in the group were directly observed by me and my research assistant and indirectly observed, during the analysis of the data, by two trained raters who were employed for the specific purpose of rating the responses on a rating scheme.[8] In many cases, there was high agreement between these direct and indirect observations. Furthermore, in most cases, the comments made by these mothers during the small-group discussions corroborated their responses on the individual questionnaires.

All eighty women who volunteered to participate in this study completed the two individual questionnaires described as part of phase one of the data collection.[9] Of this total group, fifty-three women also agreed to participate in the semistructured small-group discussions. Each small group was composed of at least eight and no more than twelve early- or late-timing mothers. There were six groups in all—three groups of early-timing mothers and three groups of late-timing mothers.

During each group discussion, I invited each woman to introduce herself and to state anything about herself that she wished to share with the group, including the ages of her children. This technique of "going around the group" at the very beginning helped make the women feel more comfortable sharing with and listening to one another. It is usually easier for individuals to participate more freely in a group discussion if they have an opportunity to share at the beginning of a session.

Following these introductions, I asked a standard set of questions during each group session to ensure that each group of mothers was provided with a similar set of stimuli, to which they could respond in any way they chose. The questions were designed as a springboard for an open discussion, but they provided enough structure to keep things balanced and moving. These questions grew out of my goals for the study and from the pilot study that had preceded this more formal study. Participants were asked to discuss (1) the most pleasurable and frustrating experiences of motherhood; (2) the advantages and disadvantages of having children when they did; (3) the ways in which motherhood had most changed their lives; (4) how they balanced or juggled their own needs and those of their children, and (5) how much emotional support they received from their families.

Individual Questionnaires

There are problems with the reliability or accuracy of data collected in small groups, including a limitation known as "social desirability." That is, there may be a tendency for group participants to agree with one another rather than to express their own opinions. Sometimes, group participants are afraid to reveal feelings or experiences that may be viewed by the group as different from what other members are expressing. To counterbalance this problem—and to provide a method of cross-validation whereby the qualitative data from the small-group discussions could be checked against another measure—a thirteen-page individual questionnaire was constructed.[10] Before participating in a small-group discussion, each mother completed one of these questionnaires as well as an Adjective Checklist to Describe Personality—a forced-choice standardized instrument consisting of eighty-eight adjectives grouped into eleven scales.[11] These two individual, self-reporting instruments provided a way for each woman to respond to specific sets of standardized questions with any responses she felt appropriate but without being observed by others in the group.

Both the closed-ended questions on the questionnaire and the numerical response obtained from the Adjective Checklist were easy for the mothers to comprehend without detailed instructions. The use of these methods also encouraged the participants to provide more concrete responses, which could be more easily measured and statistically analyzed by computer.[12] The limitations of this individual approach are that responses to instruments administered by mail are necessarily more superficial than those elicited in personal group interviews. During the group sessions, I and the other women in the group could ask questions or make comments that related to other mothers' responses.

This study was designed so that in-depth material (quotations from the women who participated in the group discussions) would buttress the statistical findings to present a more comprehensive perspective of the experiences women have as mothers. The more subjective but very interesting and rich qualitative data were also corroborated or refuted by the statistical findings. In this way, the assets of one method of data collection and analysis helped counterbalance the weaknesses of the other method. However, the degree to which the results can be generalized is limited because of the effect of other important intervening variables (socioeconomic status, education), the self-selected nature of the sample, and the exploratory design of the research project.

Table 1
Description of Study Population by Important Demographic Variables

	Early-Timing Mothers	Late-Timing Mothers
Current mean age (yrs)	26.8	34.8
Mean age at birth of first child (yrs)	23.0	32.0
Mean number of years married	5.5	7.5
Mean number of years worked prior to having children	3.5	9.0
Percentage working outside the home after the birth of children	59.7	59.0
Percentage currently working outside the home	25.7	46.0
Percentage working full-time	2.6	8.8
Percentage college graduates	25.6	97.4
Number of children (mode)	2	1
Current mean family income	$25,000–30,000	$35,000–45,000

Table 2
List of Personality Characteristics by Scale

Achievement	Autonomy	Endurance	Dominance
striving	self-reliant	steady	influential
enterprising	aggressive	steadfast	assertive
purposeful	independent	stable	persuasive
productive	opinionated	persevering	authoritative
achieving	individualistic	deliberate	forceful
hard-driving	outspoken	relentless	powerful
aspiring	self-sufficient	rational	dominant
initiative	adventurous	persistent	confident

Inner Turmoil	Deference	Nurturance	Social Impression
unsure	apologizing	sympathetic	proper
anxious	deferential	affectionate	seek recognition
self-doubting	subservient	helpful	well-behaved
troubled	self-subordinating	appreciative	poised
confused	obedient	comforting	make good impression
inconsistent	compliant	gentle	self-controlled
dissatisfied	yielding	supporting	seek approval
conflict-laden	submissive	warm	reasonable

Table 2 (continued)

Sentience	Play	Introspection
sensitive	jovial	introspective
romantic	carefree	questioning
sensuous	pleasure-seeking	preoccupied
alive to impressions	leisurely	probing
emotional	joking	reflective
intuitive	relaxed	insightful
tender	frivolous	philosophical
expressive	spontaneous	deep

Source: Adapted from scales developed by Barbara Reinke, "Adjective Checklist to Describe Personality." Reprinted with permission.

Table 3
Results of Adjective Checklist for Personality Characteristics as Determined by ANOVA and Chi-Square Analysis

	Mean Scores[a]		Level of Significance for F Value (ANOVA)	Level of Significance for Chi-Square Value
	Early-Timers	Late-Timers		
Achievement	3.1	3.4	$< .01^*$	$< .02^*$
Autonomy	3.2	3.3	$< .10^*$	$< .001$
Dominance	2.8	2.9	$< .50$	$< .01^*$
Endurance	3.3	3.7	$< .0000^*$	$< .01^*$
Inner turmoil	2.2	2.4	$< .10^*$	$< .10^*$
Play	2.8	2.4	$< .001^*$	$< .001^*$
Deference	2.7	2.4	$< .01^*$	$< .001^*$
Nurturance	4.0	3.9	$< .15-> .10$	$< .15-> .10$
Social impression	3.4	3.5	$< .20-> .18$	$< .15-> .10$
Introspection	3.1	3.3	$< .15-> .10$	$< .60$
Sentience	3.5	3.4	$< .50$	$< .50$

[a]Range of scores is from 1 = not at all descriptive to 5 = extremely descriptive.
*Statistically significant at $p < .10$.

Table 4
Mothers' Perceptions of Source of Identity

	Percentage Choosing Factor as Important[a]		Level of Significance for F Value (ANOVA)	Level of Significance for Chi-Square Value
	Late-Timers	Early-Timers		
Own achievements and activities	66.7	24.3	< .00001*	< .001*
Relationship with husband	18.4	56.8	< .01*	< .05*
Relationship with child/children	17.9	21.6	> .10–< .15	> .25
Perception of my parents' support of me and my role	2.8	8.6	> .35	> .60

[a]Percentages do not sum to 100 percent because some participants chose more than one factor as most important.
*Significant at p < .10.

Table 5
Factors That Influence Decisions Regarding
Work or Daily Activities

	Percentage Choosing Factor as Important[a]		Level of Significance for F Value (ANOVA)	Level of Significance for Chi-Square Value
	Late-Timers	Early-Timers		
Husband's career or attitude	7.9	7.7	> .65	> .40
Children's needs	53.8	76.9	< .10*	< .10*
Mother's own needs	48.7	23.1	.01*	< .10*
Parents/relations/ friends	11.1	2.6	> .15–< .20	> .20

[a]Percentages do not sum to 100 percent because some participants chose more than one factor as most important. ·
*Significant at p < .10.

Table 6
Degree of Satisfaction with Certain Aspects of Life

	Percentage Ranking Aspects as No. 1[a]		
	Late-Timers	Early-Timers	Level of Significance for Chi-Square Value
Relationship with child/children	56.4	36.0	.05*
Relationship with husband	38.5	48.7	> .65
Activities done by self other than paid work—e.g., cooking, sewing projects, gardening	15.4	20.5	> .40
Paid work	5.1	5.1	> .35
Relationships with friends/relatives	5.1	5.1	< .15
Unpaid activities done with others—e.g., volunteer work, clubs	2.6	0.0	> .35

[a]Percentages do not sum to 100 percent because some participants ranked more than one aspect of life as number one.

*Statistically significant at $p < .10$.

Table 7
How Mothers Spend Their Time During an Average Week

	Mean Number of Hours			
	Late-Timers	Early-Timers	Level of Significance for F Value (ANOVA)	Level of Significance for t Values (t Test)
Time spent with children other than tasks	24.0	42.4	< .01*	< .05*
Time spent working alone on goal-oriented activities	12.8	9.9	> .25	> .20
Time spent socializing with husband	14.1	17.0	> .30	> .20
Time spent doing tasks with others	11.6	11.0	> .80	> .65
Time spent socializing with friends/relatives	9.3	11.0	> .30	< .15
Time spent in goal-directed activities at paid job	11.3	3.2	< .01*	< .01*

Table 7 (continued)

	Mean Number of Hours		Level of Significance for F Value (ANOVA)	Level of Significance for t Values (t Test)
	Late-Timers	Early-Timers		
Time spent socializing at paid job	.8	.4	> .25	> .20
Education (including study time)	2.9	3.2	> .80	> .70

*Statistically significant at $p < .10$.

Notes

1. INTRODUCTION

1. The birth rate for all women aged 15–44 years was predicted to increase 8 percent between 1979 and 1985, with the largest increases at 16.3 percent for women aged 30–34 years and 26.7 percent for women aged 35–39 years. For women aged 20–24 years—traditionally one of the groups with the highest fertility rates—there actually was a predicted decrease of 1 percent! U.S. Department of Health and Human Services, *Annual Summary, 1979, Vital Statistics of the United States*. National Center for Health Statistics, 13 November 1980, p. 10; "Fertility Rate Drops Except for Women 30–34 Years Old," *New York Times*, 4 December 1985.

2. U.S. Department of Commerce, Bureau of the Census. *Population Characteristics*, Series P–20, No. 386, April 1984.

3. In chorionic villi sampling, a catheter guided by ultrasound is inserted into the uterus to withdraw a small amount of chorionic villi tissue, which surrounds the fetus and later becomes the placenta. This procedure may be an excellent alternative to amniocentesis because it can be done from the eighth through the twelfth week of pregnancy and results are available within two weeks. "Fetal Health: New Early Diagnosis Studies," *New York Times*, 9 March 1985, p. 15.

4. Women who decide not to marry during early adulthood or who plan to have no children during this period become more involved in a career or work interest than those who marry and plan a family. According to research studies:

   The timing of marriage, childbearing, education and work have long term implications for the life patterns of women. . . . Developmental change may also result from the experience, sense of competence and status gained in the work world of a woman who does delay childbearing.

   Aletha Stein and Ann Higgins-Trenk, "Development of Families from Childhood through Adulthood: Career and Feminine Role Orientations" in *Life Span Development and Behavior*, ed. Paul Baltes (New York: Academic Press, 1978), p. 278.

5. Daniel Levinson et al., *The Seasons of a Man's Life* (New York: Ballantine Books, 1979).

6. Alice Rossi, "Transition to Parenthood," *Journal of Marriage and the Family*, 30(February 1968):26.

7. Wellesley College Center for Research on Women, *Research Report*, Vol. 4, no. 2 (Wellesley, Mass.: Wellesley College, 1985).

8. Andras Angyal, *Neurosis and Treatment: A Holistic Theory* (New York: Wiley, 1965), p. 29.

9. Because of limitations in the methodology, such as a self-selected population and an exploratory research design, the reader is advised to view these findings as possible trends in what the mothers are experiencing. (See Appendix for further discussion).

2. THE MOTHERS: WHO THEY ARE, HOW THEY COPE

1. Erik Eriksen, "The Problem of Ego Identity," *Psychological Issues* 1(1959):102, quoted in Barbara Newman and Philip Newman, *Development Through Life: A Psychosocial Approach* (Homewood, Ill.: Dorsey Press, 1984), p. 336.
2. Agnes O'Connell, "Determinants of Women's Life Styles and Sense of Identity: Personality, Attitudes, Significant Others, and Demographic Characteristics" (Ph.D. dissertation, Rutgers—The State University of New Jersey, 1974), p. 1.
3. Andras Angyal, *Neurosis Treatment: A Holistic Theory* (New York: Wiley, 1965), pp. 4, 10, 11, 12 passim.
4. Nancy Chodorow illustrated some of the contrasts in adult life between the mode of functioning at work and the mode of functioning at home. She described work outside the home as "likely to be contractual, to be more specifically delimited, and to contain a notion of defined progression and product." This description of a work function appears similar to an authonomous mode. Nancy Chodorow, *The Reproduction of Mothering: Psychoanalysis and the Sociology of Gender* (Berkeley: University of California Press, 1978), p. 179.
5. O'Connell, "Determinants of Women's Life Styles," p. 1.
6. Angyal, *Neurosis and Treatment*, pp. 15–20.
7. David Bakan, *The Duality of Human Existence* (Chicago: Rand McNally, 1966), p. 15, quoted in Rae Carlson, "Sex Differences in Ego Functioning: Exploratory Studies of Agency and Communion," *Journal of Consulting and Clinical Psychology* 37(1971):271. Chodorow contrasts working outside the home with the wife/mother role, which she sees as having a "non-bounded quality with diffuse obligations . . . women's activities in the home involve continuous connection to and concern about children and attunement to adult masculine needs, both of which require connection to, rather than separateness from other" (Chodorow, *Reproduction of Mothering*, p. 179).
8. Chi-square and analysis of variance techniques were used for data analysis.
9. Lawrence Shulman, *The Skills of Helping: Individuals and Groups* (Itasca, Ill.: Peacock, 1979), pp. 116–117.
10. Grace Baruch and Rosalind Barnett, "On the Well-Being of Adult Women," in *Competence and Coping During Adulthood*, ed. Lynne Bond and James Rosen (Hanover, N.H.: University Press of New England, 1980), p. 254.

3. THE GRATIFICATIONS AND FRUSTRATIONS OF MOTHERHOOD

1. Margaret Mahler, F. Pine, and A. Bergman, *The Psychological Birth of The Human Infant* (New York: Basic Books, 1975); D.W. Winnicott, *The Maturational Processes and the Facilitating Environment* (New York: International Universities Press, 1965); and John MacMurray, *Persons in Relation* (Atlantic Highlands, N.J.: Humanities Press, 1961).
2. Margaret Mahler, F. Pine and A. Bergman, "The Mother's Reaction to Her Toddler's Drive for Individuation," in *Parenthood: Its Psychology and Psychopathology*, ed. Therese Benedek and James Anthony (Boston: Little, Brown, 1970), p. 259.

4: MOTHERHOOD: A BALANCING ACT

1. Theodore Lidz, *The Person: His or Her Development Throughout the Life Cycle*, rev. ed. (New York: Basic Books, 1983).
2. D.W. Winnicott, *The Maturational Processes and the Facilitating Environment* (New York: International Universities Press, 1965), pp. 44–45.
3. Helene Deutsch, *Psychology of Women: A Psychoanalytic Interpretation of Motherhood*, Vol. II. (New York: Grune and Stratton, 1945); Lidz, *The Person*; Therese Benedek, *Psychoanalytic Investigations* (New York: Quadrangle, 1973).
4. Lucie Jessner, E. Weigert, and J. Foy, "The Development of Parental Attitudes During Pregnancy," in *Parenthood: Its Psychology and Psychopathology*, ed. Therese Benedek and James Anthony (Boston: Little, Brown, 1979), p. 220.
5. Grace Baruch, Rosalind Barnett, and Caryl Rivers, *Lifeprints: New Patterns of Love and Work for Today's Women*, (New York: McGraw-Hill, 1983), p. 14.
6. Therese Benedek, "Motherhood and Nurturing," in *Parenthood: Its Psychology and Psychopathology*, ed. Therese Benedek and James Anthony (Boston: Little, Brown, 1970); Heinz Lichtenstein, *The Dilemma of Human Identity*, (New York: Jason Aronson, 1977); Winnicott, *The Maturational Processes*.
7. Benedek, "Motherhood and Nurturing," p. 165.
8. Lichtenstein, *Dilemma of Human Identity*, p. 77.
9. Benedek, *Psychoanalytic Investigations*, p. 279.
10. Ibid.
11. Ibid.
12. The quality of mothering was evaluated by observing the mother's interaction with the baby and was assessed on a number of subscales, including the mother's acceptance of her infant, her sensitivity to the baby's needs, and her "apparent affect while she was handling the baby." The researchers also conducted extensive clinical interviews in which they investigated "the mother's feelings about her child and how well she felt she was coping with the baby." F.K. Grossman, L.S. Eichler, and S.A. Winickoff, *Pregnancy, Birth and Parenthood* (San Francisco: Jossey-Bass, 1980), p. 103.
13. These researchers cautioned their readers that further investigation was necessary to determine whether the latter style is less adaptive at later stages of childrearing. Ibid., p. 106.
14. Lidz, *The Person*, p. 364.

5. A MOTHER'S DILEMMA: MEETING HER OWN NEEDS AND HER CHILD'S NEEDS

1. Terry Carrilio and Carolyn Walter, "Mirroring and Autonomy: The Dual Tasks of Mothers," *Child and Adolescent Social Work Journal*, 3 (Fall 1984):143.
2. Daniel Levinson et al., *The Seasons of a Man's Life* (New York: Ballantine Books, 1979).
3. George Valliant, *Adaptation to Life* (Boston: Little, Brown, 1977).
4. Carol Gilligan, *In a Different Voice* (Cambridge, Mass.: Harvard University Press, 1982).
5. Ibid., p. 155.
6. Gilligan, *In a Different Voice*; Jean Baker Miller, *Toward a New Psychology of Women* (Boston: Beacon Press, 1976); Lillian Rubin, *Intimate Strangers: Men and Women Together* (New York: Harper and Row, 1983).
7. Nancy Chodorow, *The Reproduction of Mothering: Psychoanalysis and the Sociology of Gender* (Berkeley: University of California Press, 1978), p. 167.

8. Rubin, *Intimate Strangers*, pp. 56, 58.
9. Gilligan, *In a Different Voice*, p. 22.
10. Gilligan, *In a Different Voice*; Miller, *Toward a Psychology of Women*; Judith Bardwick, "The Seasons of a Woman's Life," in *Women's Lives: New Theory, Research and Policy*, ed. D.G. McGuigan (Ann Arbor: University of Michigan, Center for Continuing Education for Women, 1980).
11. Miller, *Toward a Psychology of Women*, p. 110.
12. Elaine Heffner, *Mothering: The Emotional Experience of Motherhood After Freud and Feminism* (New York: Doubleday–Anchor, 1980), p. 45.
13. Ibid., p. 171.
14. J.E. Marcia, "Development and Validation of Ego Identity Status," *Journal of Personality and Social Psychology* 3(1966):551–58, quoted in Barbara Newman and Philip Newman, *Development Through Life: A Psychosocial Approach* (Homewood, Ill.: Dorsey Press, 1984), p. 338.
15. Deane Foltz, "Postponement of the First Birth: Patterns of Childbearing in an Educated Group of Women," (Ph.D. dissertation, University of Michigan, 1981), p. 129.
16. Grace Baruch, Rosalind Barnett, and Caryl Rivers, *Lifeprints: New Patterns of Love and Work for Today's Women* (New York: McGraw-Hill, 1983), p. 241.
17. Of the twenty-two late-timing mothers who ranked the activities in this way, ten work outside the home, ten are homemakers, and two are students. Since 46 percent of the total group of late-timing mothers within this study work outside the home and 46 percent are homemakers (the remainder are students), there does not seem to be anything unusual about the group that ranked degree of satisfaction with relationships with children as number one.
18. The results of both early and late-timing responses were subjected to analysis of variance and t-test to determine where there might be significant differences between the means of the two groups.
19. When "Time spent with children" was entered as a dependent variable, partializing out the effects of hours worked, there was still a significant difference between the two groups for hours spent with children ($p < .02$).
20. Miller, *Toward a Psychology of Women*, p. 71.
21. Baruch et al., *Lifeprints*, p. 30.

6. A MOTHER'S SUPPORT SYSTEM: FRIENDS, PARENTS, AND HUSBAND

1. Carol Anderson, "Community Connection: The Impact of Social Networks on Family and Individual Functioning," in *Normal Family Processes*, ed. Fromma Walsh (New York: Guilford Press, 1982), pp. 425–26.
2. Brent Miller and Judith Myers-Walls, "Parenthood: Stresses and Coping Strategies," in *Stress and the Family: Coping with Normative Transitions*, Vol. 1, ed. Hamilton McCubbin and Charles Figley (New York: Brunner/Mazel, 1983), p. 69.
3. *Baltimore Sun*, "Can She Have It All: Women Putting Careers on Hold to Start Families," 27 March 1985, p. 29.
4. During the pilot phase of this research project, I included questions regarding the woman's relationship with her mother, but I deleted them later because of the length of the instrument.
5. F.K. Grossman, L. S. Eichler, and S.A. Winickoff, *Pregnancy, Birth and Parenthood* (San Francisco: Jossey-Bass, 1980), p. 43.
6. Readers who are interested in this subject are referred to Pamela Daniels and Kathy Weingarten, *Sooner or Later: The Timing of Parenthood* (New York: Norton, 1982), which focuses on the marital relationship.

7. Theodore Lidz, *The Person: His or Her Development Throughout the Life Cycle,* Rev. ed. (New York: Basic Books, 1983).
8. These data support the research of Daniels and Weingarten, who found similar patterns in early and late-timing families. Daniels and Weingarten, *Sooner or Later,* p. 71.

7. THE ULTIMATE JUGGLING ACT: WORK AND MOTHERHOOD

1. Wendy Stewart, "A Psychosocial Study of the Formation of the Early Adult Life Structure in Women" (Ph.D. dissertation, Columbia University, 1976), pp. 99–101 passim.
2. Deane Foltz, "Postponement of the First Birth: Patterns of Childbearing in an Educated Group of Women" (Ph.D. dissertation, University of Michigan, 1981), p. 130.
3. Pamela Daniels and Kathy Weingarten, *Sooner or Later: The Timing of Parenthood in Adult Lives* (New York: Norton, 1982), p. 128.
4. Linda Wolfe, "Mommy's 39, Daddy's 57 — And Baby Was Just Born," *New York Magazine,* 5 April 1982, p. 29. Reprinted by permission.
5. Anita Schreve, "Careers and the Lure of Motherhood," *New York Times Magazine,* 21 November 1982, p. 43. Copyright © 1982 by The New York Times Company. Reprinted by permission.
6. Ibid. Copyright © 1982 by The New York Times Company. Reprinted by permission.
7. "The New Dropouts: Career Women," *Philadelphia Inquirer,* 10 March 1985, Section F, pp. 1, 11.
8. This difficulty in adjusting to parenthood has also been reported by other researchers. See Daniels and Weingarten, *Sooner or Later;* and Alice Rossi, "Life Span Theories and Women's Lives," *Signs: Journal of Women in Culture and Society* 6, no. 1(1980):5–32.

8. THE MOTHERS SPEAK OUT: THE ADVANTAGES AND DISADVANTAGES OF TIMING

1. Because this material is a discussion of general ideas and is not so specific with regard to the women's behavior, it was not included in the formal content analysis of the research project. However, it is interesting, and it confirms other discussions in this book and provides additional material regarding what is gratifying and frustrating about motherhood.

9. PARENTHOOD: AN OPPORTUNITY TO DEVELOP AS AN ADULT

1. One recent addition to research in this area is Andrea Boroff Eagan, *The Newborn Mother: Stages of Her Growth* (New York: Little, Brown, 1985).
2. Daniel Levinson et al., *The Seasons of a Man's Life* (New York: Ballantine Books, 1979).
3. "Women Battle to Balance Babies, Business," *NASW News* 28, no. 10 (November 1982):1.
4. Therese Benedek, "The Psychobiology of Pregnancy," in *Parenthood: Its Psychology and Psychopathology,* ed. Therese Benedek and James Anthony (Boston: Little, Brown, 1979), p. 143.
5. Judith Bardwick, *The Psychology of Women: A Study of Bio Cultural Conflicts* (New York: Harper and Row, 1971), p. 212.
6. Therese Benedek, *Psychoanalytic Investigations* (New York: Quadrangle, 1973), p. 385; Margaret Mahler, F. Pine, and A. Bergman, "The Mother's Reaction to her Toddler's Drive for Individuation," in *Parenthood: Its Psychology and Psychopathology,* ed. Therese Benedek and James Anthony (Boston: Little, Brown, 1970).

7. Alice Rossi, "Transition to Parenthood," *Journal of Marriage and the Family*, 30 (February 1968):29.
8. Bardwick, *Psychology of Women*, p. 212.
9. However, neither early- nor late-timing mothers reported a decrease in self-esteem following motherhood.
10. Barbara Newman and Philip Newman, *Development Through Life: A Psychosocial Approach* (Homewood, Ill.: Dorsey Press, 1984), p. 457.
11. Deane Foltz, "Postponement of the First Birth: Patterns of Childbearing in an Educated Group of Women" (Ph.D. dissertation, University of Michigan, 1981), p. 123.
12. Alice Rossi, "Life-Span Theories and Women's Lives," *Signs: Journal of Women in Culture and Society* 6, no. 1(1980): 25, 26.
13. Naomi Munson, "Having Babies Again," *Commentary* 71 (April 1981):60.
14. Benedek, *Psychoanalytic Investigations*, p. 385.

10. CONCLUSIONS

1. Theodore Lidz, *The Person: His or Her Development Throughout the Life Cycle*, Rev. ed. (New York: Basic Books, 1983), pp. 57, 58, 59.
2. Therese Benedek, *Psychoanalytic Investigations* (New York: Quadrangle, 1973); Lidz, *The Person*.
3. Miriam Polster and Erving Polster, *Gestalt Therapy Integrated* (New York: Vintage Books, 1974), pp. 92–97.
4. Julie Jenks, "The Mystery of Women's Early Development," *Clinical Social Work Journal* 11(Spring 1983):59; Wendy Stewart, "A Psychosocial Study of the Formation of the Early Adult Life Structure in Women" (Ph.D. dissertation, Columbia University, 1976).

APPENDIX

1. Pamela Daniels and Kathy Weingarten, *Sooner or Later: The Timing of Parenthood in Adult Lives* (New York: Norton, 1982); Deane Foltz, "Postponement of the First Birth: Patterns of Childbearing in an Educated Group of Women" (Ph.D. dissertation, University of Michigan, 1981); "Can She Have It All? Women Putting Careers on Hold to Start Families," *The Baltimore Sun*, 27 March 1985; Anita Shreve, "Careers and the Lure of Motherhood," *New York Times Magazine*, 21 November 1982.
2. U.S. Department of Commerce, Bureau of the Census, *Current Population Reports, Population Characteristics*, Series P-20, No. 379, May 1983, p. 5.
3. Ibid.
4. Ibid.
5. Ibid.
6. In precoding the responses, the researcher followed rules for content analysis and determined that each unit of analysis was an "utterance"—a complete statement made by one participant before another participant spoke. Donald Kiesler, *The Process of Psychotherapy: Empirical Foundation and Systems of Analysis* (Chicago: Aldine, 1973), p. 51.
7. The two raters, working independently, achieved interrater reliability scores ranging from .6658 to .9158, obtained by Pearson's product moment correlation.
8. In surveying the literature, I was unable to locate an appropriate standardized scale to measure the concepts I was interested in studying. Therefore, to measure the degree of comfort/discomfort that the women in this study experienced with the dimensions of autonomy and merging—both within their adult lives and in relationship with their children—the researcher developed a rating scheme. In constructing the set of scales for the

rating scheme, the researcher wanted to create an instrument that would obtain an evaluation or quantitative judgment of the degree to which the participants' responses (to open-ended questions on the questionnaire and during the small-group discussions) reflected the theoretical constructs conceptualized by the statements within the scales on the rating scheme.

Each rater placed the response being rated on a 7-point rating scale with intervals that appeared to be equal. A numerical value was attached to each point or category. Apparently equal intervals were selected so that the data could be subjected to statistics appropriate for interval data, such as the mean and analysis of variance (ANOVA). The researcher followed instructions for construction of scales in Delbert C. Miller, *Handbook of Research Design and Social Measurement* (New York: Longman, 1977); and Claire Selltitz, Lawrence Wrightsman, and Stuart Cook, *Research Methods in Social Relations* (New York: Holt, Rinehart and Winston, 1976).

In the initial drafts of the rating scheme, the statements consisted of a complex combination of phenomena that were not easily understood by colleages or by the research assistant who had helped collect the data. With more effort, the researcher finally arrived at a scheme in which the statements anchoring the scales described a more directly observable indicator that could be used as a cue by the raters. With each revision of the rating scheme the researcher attempted to (1) present clear polar opposites within statements anchoring each end of the scales; (2) keep scales as unidimensional as possible; and (3) create statements that would be as representative as possible of the theoretical constructs under study.

There are limitations to the final rating scheme adopted, especially in creating clear polar opposites as anchor statements for each end of the autonomy–merging (self–other) continuum. The final rating scheme used by the raters consisted of such statements as "I feel in charge of my life and/or my time" at one end of the scale and "My life and/or my time seem to be primarily determined by others" at the other end. Descriptive adjectives, such as "very reflective" or "somewhat reflective," were used to define different points on the continuum so that what was represented by a certain point on the scale was clear to the raters.

To prevent response bias on the part of the raters as much as possible, the positive pole or high end of the scale (merging) and the negative pole or low end of the scale (autonomy) were alternated on the form of the rating scheme. For purposes of coding and analysis of the data, however, these poles were not alternated.

It was the researcher's intention that each statement on the rating scheme would serve as a visual cue for the raters, so that they could choose the scale that was most reflective of the response from the transcript as they listened to the audio tape and read the written transcript of each group session.

9. Only seventy-eight of these responses were scored; two of the original volunteers did not fit the requirements of the study because of the age of their children and the mothers' ages at the birth of their first children.

10. This questionnaire for mothers, designed by the researcher, was composed of both open-ended and forced-choice questions (using a Likert-type scale and a 10-point rating scale). The questions tapped seven categories, most of which corresond to the categories of questions asked of the women who participated in the small-group discussions: (1) sense of identity and self-esteem; (2) relationship with children—gratifications and frustrations, degree of comfort/discomfort with various aspects of motherhood; (3) advantages and disadvantages to the timing of parenthood; (4) how time is spent and prioritized; (5) levels of satisfaction with various aspects of life; (6) adjustment to motherhood—ways in which parenthood has changed the woman's life; and (7) support systems.

11. The Adjective Checklist to Describe Personality Characteristics was developed by Bar-

bara Reinke, "Psychosocial Changes Among Women from Early Adulthood to Midlife as a Function of Chronological Age and Family Life Cycle Phase" (Ph.D. Dissertation, University of Kansas, 1982.) Reinke developed this checklist by using adjectives from scales measuring achievement, autonomy, deference, dominance, endurance, nurturance, and play on Gough's Adjective Checklist and Jackson's Personality Research Form. The remaining three scales were constructed by Reinke to measure self-perceived inner turmoil, tendencies toward introspection, and interest in making a favorable social impression. Table A–2 provides Reinke's list of adjectives.

12. Data from forced-choice questions and ratings by trained raters were subjected to computer analysis (using SPSS for crosstabs and BMDP Statistical Packages). Initially, a detailed data description was obtained, including frequencies, to observe general trends in the data. Significant differences in frequency were obtained via chi-square analysis for ordinal data, and significant differences in means were obtained via analysis of variance and *t*-test. Analysis of covariance was also used when appropriate.

References and Bibliography

Abarbamel, Alice. "Redefining Motherhood." In *The Future of the Family*, edited by Louise K. Howe, pp. 349–67. New York: Simon and Schuster, 1972.

Anderson, Carol. "Community Connection: The Impact of Social Networks on Family and Individual Functioning." In *Normal Family Processes*, edited by Fromma Walsh, pp. 425–45. New York: Guilford Press, 1982.

Angyal, Andras. *Neurosis and Treatment: A Holistic Theory.* New York: Wiley, 1965.

Bailey, Kenneth. *Methods of Social Research.* New York: Free Press, 1978.

Bakan, David. *The Duality of Human Existence.* Chicago: Rand McNally, 1966.

Bardwick, Judith. *The Psychology of Women: A Study of Bio Cultural Conflicts.* New York: Harper and Row, 1971.

————. "The Seasons of a Woman's Life." In *Women's Lives: New Theory, Research and Policy*, edited by D.G. McGuigan. Ann Arbor: University of Michigan, Center for Continuing Education for Women, 1980.

Baruch, Grace, and Barnett, Rosalind. *The Competent Woman.* New York: Irvington, 1980.

————. "On the Well-Being of Adult Women." In *Competence and Coping During Adulthood*, edited by Lynne Bond and James Rosen, pp. 240–57. Hanover, N.H.: University Press of New England, 1980.

Baruch, Grace; Barnett, Rosaland; Rivers, Caryl. *Lifeprints: New Patterns of Love and Work for Today's Women.* New York: McGraw-Hill, 1983.

Benedek, Therese. "Motherhood and Nurturing." In *Parenthood: Its Psychology and Psychopathology*, edited by Therese Benedek and James Anthony, pp. 153–66. Boston: Little, Brown, 1970.

————. "Parenthood During the Life Cycle." In *Parenthood: Its Psychology and Psychopathology*, pp. 185–206. Edited by Therese Benedek and James Anthony. Boston: Little, Brown, 1970.

————. "The Psychobiology of Pregnancy." In *Parenthood: Its Psychology and Psychopathology*, edited by Therese Benedek and James Anthony, pp. 137–54. Boston: Little, Brown, 1970.

————. *Psychoanalytic Investigations.* New York: Quadrangle, 1973.

Bennett, Nancy; Biefer, J.; Conrad, J.; Grossman, A.; Harding, S.; Powers, J.; Rentschler, P.; Wahl, M.; and Warren, S. "Juggling Contradictions: Women's Ideas about Families." Social Science Research Community at the Residential College, University of Michigan, Ann Arbor, 1979. Mimeographed.

Bibring, Grete; Dwyer, T.; Huntingdon, D.; and Valenstein, A. "A Study of the Psychological Processes in Pregnancy and of the Earliest Mother-Child Relationship." *Psychoanalytic Study of the Child* 16(1961):9–27.

Blaylock, Hubert. *Social Statistics.* Rev. 2d ed. New York: McGraw-Hill, 1979.

Brennan, Eileen. "Viewing Depressed Women through a Developmental Model." Paper presented at the Annual Program Meeting of the Council on Social Work Education, New York, 8 March 1982.

Brennan, Eileen, and Weik, Ann. "Theories of Adult Development: Creating a Context for Practice." *Social Casework* 62(January 181):13–19.

Carlson, Rae. "Sex Differences in Ego Functioning: Exploratory Studies of Agency and Communion." *Journal of Consulting and Clinical Psychology* 37(1971):267–77.

———. "Understanding Women: Implications for Personality Theory and Research." *Journal of Social Issues* 28, No. 2(1972):17–32.

Carrilio, Terry, and Walter, Carolyn. "Mirroring and Autonomy: The Dual Tasks of Mothers." *Child and Adolescent Social Work Journal* 3(Fall 1984):143–152.

Chodorow, Nancy. *The Reproduction of Mothering: Psychoanalysis and the Sociology of Gender.* Berkeley: University of California Press, 1978.

Cohen, Mabel Blake. "Personal Identity and Sexual Identity." *Psychiatry* 29, No. 1(1966): 1–14.

Daniels, Pamela, and Weingarten, Kathy. *Sooner or Later: The Timing of Parenthood in Adult Lives.* New York: Norton, 1982.

Davis, Madeline, and Wallbridge, David. *Boundary and Space: An Introduction to the Work of D.W. Winnicott.* New York: Brunner/Mazel, 1981.

Deutsch, Helene, M.D. *Psychology of Women: A Psychoanalytic Interpretation of Motherhood.* Vol. II. New York: Grune and Stratton, 1945.

Deutscher, Max. "Brief Family Therapy in the Course of the First Pregnancy: A Clinical Note." *Contemporary Psychoanalysis* 7 (1970–71):21–35.

Dixon, W.J., ed. *BMDP Statistical Software Manual.* Berkeley: University of California Press, 1982.

Eagan, Andrea Boroff. *The Newborn Mother: Stages of Her Growth.* Boston: Little, Brown, 1985.

Eisenbaum, Luise, and Orbach, Susie. *Understanding Women: A Feminist Approach.* New York: Basic Books, 1982.

Eriksen, Erik. "The Problem of Ego Identity," *Psychological Issues* 1(1959):102.

Foltz, Deane. "Postponement of the First Birth: Patterns of Childbearing in an Educated Group of Women." Ph.D. dissertation, University of Michigan, 1981.

Gilligan, Carol. *In a Different Voice.* Cambridge, Mass.: Harvard University Press, 1982.

———. "New Maps of Development—New Visions of Maturity." *American Journal of Orthopsychiatry* 52(April 1982):199–212.

Gornick, Vivian, and Moran, Barbara, eds. *Women in a Sexist Society.* New York: Basic Books, 1971.

Grossman, F.K.; Eichler, L.S.; and Winickoff, S.A. *Pregnancy, Birth and Parenthood.* San Francisco: Jossey-Bass, 1980.

Gutmann, David. "Women and the Conception of Ego Strength." *Merrill Palmer Quarterly* 11(July 1965):229–40.

———. "Parenthood: A Key to the Comparative Study of the Life Cycle." In *Life Span Developmental Psychology: Normative Life Crisis,* edited by Nancy Datan and Leon Ginsberg, pp. 168–80. New York: Academic Press, 1975.

Heffner, Elaine. *Mothering: The Emotional Experience of Motherhood After Freud and Feminism.* New York: Doubleday–Anchor, 1980.

Jenks, Julie. "The Mystery of Women's Early Development." *Clinical Social Work Journal* 11(Spring 1983):52–63.

Jessner, Lucie; Weigert, E.; and Foy, J. "The Development of Parental Attitudes During Pregnancy." In *Parenthood: Its Psychology and Psychopathology,* edited by Therese Benedek and James Anthony, pp. 209–44. Boston: Little, Brown, 1970.

Kerlinger, Fred. *Foundations of Behavioral Research.* New York: Holt, Rinehart and Winston, 1964.

Kestenberg, J.S. "On the Development of Maternal Feelings in Early Childhood." *Psychoanalytical Study of the Child* 11(1965):257–91.

Kiesler, Donald. *The Process of Psychotherapy: Empirical Foundation and Systems of Analysis.* Chicago: Aldine, 1973.

Leifer, Myra. "Psychological Changes Accompanying Pregnancy and Motherhood." *Genetic Psychology Monograph* 95(February 1977):55–96.

Levinson, Daniel. "Four Perspectives on the Adult Life Course." *Yale Psychiatry Quarterly* 2(Winter 1980):2–14.

Levinson, Daniel; Darrow, C.; Klein, E.; Levinson, M.; and McKee, B. *The Seasons of a Man's Life.* New York: Ballantine Books, 1979.

Lichtenstein, Heinz. *The Dilemma of Human Identity.* New York: Jason Aronson, 1977.

Lidz, Theodore. *The Person: His or Her Development Throughout the Life Cycle.* Rev. ed. New York: Basic Books, 1983.

Macmurray, John. *Persons in Relation.* Atlantic Highlands, N.J.: Humanities Press, 1961.

Mahler, Margaret; Pine, F.; and Bergman, A. "The Mother's Reaction to Her Toddler's Drive for Individuation." In *Parenthood: Its Psychology and Psychopathology,* edited by Therese Benedek and James Anthony, pp. 257–74. Boston: Little, Brown, 1970.

————. *The Psychological Birth of the Human Infant.* New York: Basic Books, 1975.

Marcia, J.E. "Development and Validation of Ego Identity Status," *Journal of Personality and Social Psychology* 3(1966):551–58.

Marcia, James, and Friedman, Meredith. "Ego Identity Status in College Women." *Journal of Personality* 38(1970):249–63.

McBride, A.B. *The Growth and Development of Mothers.* New York: Harper and Row, 1973.

Mednick, Martha; Tangri, Sandra; and Hoffman, Lois, eds. *Women and Achievement.* Washington, D.C.: Wiley, 1975.

Miller, Alice. *Prisoners of Childhood: The Drama of the Gifted Child and the Search for the True Self.* New York: Basic Books, 1981.

Miller, Brent, and Myers-Walls, Judith. "Parenthood: Stresses and Coping Strategies." In *Stress and the Family: Coping with Normative Transitions,* edited by Hamilton McCubbin and Charles Figley, Vol. 1, pp. 54–73. New York: Brunner/Mazel, 1983.

Miller, Delbert C. *Handbook of Research Design and Social Measurement.* New York: Longman, 1977.

Miller, Jean Baker. *Toward a New Psychology of Women.* Boston: Beacon Press, 1976.

Munson, Naomi. "Having Babies Again." *Commentary* 71 (April 1981):60–68.

Neugarten, Bernice. "Adaptation and the Life Cycle." *Counseling Psychologist* 6, No. 1(1976): 16–20.

Newman, Barbara, and Newman, Philip. *Development Through Life: A Psychosocial Approach.* Homewood, Ill.: Dorsey Press, 1984.

Nie, N.; Hull, C.; Jenkins, J.; Steinbrenner, K.; and Bent, Dale, eds. *Statistical Package for the Social Sciences.* 2d ed. New York: McGraw-Hill, 1975.

O'Connell, Agnes. "Determinants of Women's Life Styles and Sense of Identity: Personality, Attitudes, Significant Others, and Demographic Characteristics." Ph.D. dissertation, Rutgers—The State University of New Jersey, 1974.

Parens, Henry, M.D. "Parenthood as a Developmental Phase." *Journal of the American Psychoanalytic Association* 23(1975):154–65.

Plunkett, Marcia, and Weintraub, Sara. "Working Mothers of Young Children: A Study of Conflict and Integration." Ph.D. dissertation, University of Michigan, 1980.

Polansky, Norman A. *Social Work Research.* Chicago: University of Chicago Press, 1960.

Polster, Miriam, and Polster, Erving. *Gestalt Therapy Integrated.* New York: Vintage Books, 1974.

Rapoport, R.; Rapoport, R.N.; and Strelitz, Z. *Fathers, Mothers and Society.* New York: Basic Books, 1977.

Reed, J.D. "The Baby Boom." *Time,* 22 February 1982, pp. 52–59.

Reinke, Barbara. "Psychosocial Changes Among Women from Early Adulthood to Midlife as a Function of Chronological Age and Family Cycle Phase." Ph.D. dissertation, University of Kansas, 1982.

Rossi, Alice. "Transition to Parenthood." *Journal of Marriage and the Family* 30(February 1968):26–39.

———. "Life Span Theories and Women's Lives." *Signs: Journal of Women in Culture and Society* 6, No. 1(1980):5–32.

Rubin, Lillian. *Intimate Strangers: Men and Women Together.* New York: Harper and Row, 1983.

Russell, Candyce Smith. "Transition to Parenthood: Problems and Gratifications." *Journal of Marriage and the Family* 36(May 1974):294–302.

Russo, Nancy. "Overview: Sex Roles, Fertility and the Motherhood Mandate." *Psychology of Women Quarterly* 4(Fall 1979):7–15.

Salvatore, Ellen. "Mid-Life Parenthood: Implications for Social Work Practice." Paper presented at the National Association of Social Workers Symposium, Washington, D.C. 20 November 1983.

Scarf, Maggie. *Unfinished Business: Pressure Points in the Lives of Women.* New York: Doubleday, 1980.

Schecter, David, and Corman, Harvey. "The Birth of a Family: Some Early Developments in Parent–Child Interactions." *Contemporary Psychoanalysis* 15(1979):380–406.

Selltitz, Claire; Wrightsman, Lawrence; and Cook, Stuart. *Research Methods in Social Relations.* New York: Holt, Rinehart and Winston, 1976.

Shreve, Anita. "Careers and the Lure of Motherhood." *New York Times Magazine,* 21 November 1982, pp. 38–57.

Shulman, Lawrence. *The Skills of Helping: Individuals and Groups.* Itasca, Ill.: Peacock, 1979.

Smelser, Neil, and Erikson, Erik, eds. *Themes of Love and Work in Adulthood.* Cambridge, Mass.: Harvard University Press, 1980.

Stein, Aletha, and Higgins-Trenk, Ann. "Development of Families from Childhood through Adulthood: Career and Feminine Role Orientations." In *Life Span Development and Behavior,* edited by Paul Baltes, pp. 258–90. New York: Academic Press, 1968.

Stewart, Abigail, and Winter, David. "Self-Definition and Social Definition in Women." *Journal of Personality* 42(1974):239–57.

Stewart, Wendy. "A Psychosocial Study of the Formation of the Early Adult Life Structure in Women." Ph.D. dissertation, Columbia University, 1976.

U.S. Department of Commerce. Bureau of the Census. *Current Population Reports, Population Characteristics,* Series P-20, No. 379, May 1983.

U.S. Department of Commerce. Bureau of the Census. *Current Population Reports, Population Characteristics,* Series P-20, No. 386, April 1984.

U.S. Department of Health and Human Services. *Annual Summary, 1979, Vital Statistics of the United States.* Washington, D.C.: National Center for Health Statistics, 13 November 1980.

Valliant, George. *Adaptation to Life.* Boston: Little, Brown, 1977.

Walker, Lilly, and Walker, James. "Trait Anxiety in Mothers: Differences Associated with Employment Status, Family Size and Aged Children." *Psychological Reports* 47(1980):295–99.

Walstedt, Joyce Jennings. "The Altruistic Other Orientation: An Exploration of Female Powerlessness." *Psychology of Women Quarterly* 2(Winter 1977):162–75.

Wellesley College Center for Research on Women. *Research Report.* Vol. 4, No. 2. Wellesley, Mass.: Wellesley College, 1985.

Winnicott, D.W. *The Maturational Processes and the Facilitating Environment.* New York: International Universities Press, 1965.

Wolfe, Linda. "Mommy's 39, Daddy's 57 — And Baby Was Just Born." *New York Magazine,* 5 April 1982, pp. 28–34.

"Women Battle to Balance Babies, Business." *NASW News* 28 (November 1983):1, 4.

Young-Eisendrath, Pauline, and Eisendrath, Craig, R. "Where's Mother Now?" *Psychological Perspectives* 11(Spring 1980):70–82.

Index

About the Author

C AROLYN AMBLER WALTER, an assistant professor in the University of Maryland School of Social Work and Community Planning and a clinical social worker, has been focusing on women's lives and adult development issues in her writing and clinical practice for more than thirteen years. She received her Ph.D. from Bryn Mawr College Graduate School of Social Work and Social Research.

DATE DUE

1/13/88		
4 7 89	Reserve (FC)	
SEP 0 4 1991		
DEC 0 9 1992		
DEC 0 7 1993		
MAY 1 0 1995		
DEC 1 2 1995		
FEB 2 5 1997		
MAY 0 6 1998		
DEC 1 5 2000		